IT HAPPENED
IN
BASEBALL

Also by Brian McFarlane

IT HAPPENED
IN
BASEBALL

Amazing Tales from the Fields of Dreams

Brian McFarlane

Foreword by Paul Beeston
President, Toronto Blue Jays

Stoddart

First published in 1993 by
Stoddart Publishing Co. Limited
34 Lesmill Road
Toronto, Canada
M3B 2T6
(416) 445-3333

Canadian Cataloguing in Publication Data

McFarlane, Brian, 1931-
It happened in baseball: amazing tales
from the fields of dreams

ISBN 0-7737-5570-5

1. Baseball — History — Miscellanea.   I. Title.

GV867.3.M33 1993   796.357′09   C92-095637-8

Cover Design: Brant Cowie/ArtPlus Limited
Typesetting: Tony Gordon Ltd.
Printed and bound in Canada

*Stoddart Publishing gratefully acknowledges the
support of the Canada Council, Ontario Ministry of
Culture and Communications, Ontario Arts Council,
and Ontario Publishing Centre in the development of
writing and publishing in Canada.*

*T*he words ahead are dedicated to a grand group of ball players who electrified the world of baseball last October. Millions of fans, including a Canadian astronaut whooping it up in orbit, thrilled to a tense, nail-biting finish to a dramatic, never-to-be-forgotten World Series victory by the Toronto Blue Jays over the Atlanta Braves.

So one more tip of the ball cap goes to the astute front office management team of Paul Beeston and Pat Gillick, to that classy gentleman, field manager Cito Gaston, who made all the right moves, to versatile Joe Carter, who started at three different positions in the series, to Devon White, for his spectacular catch high against the wall in game four, to boyish-looking Pat Borders whose torrid hitting brought him the Series' MVP award, to Juan Guzman, Roberto Alomar, Tom Henke, Jimmy Key, and the rest of the Jays. And especially to Dave Winfield, the oldest Blue Jay at 41, whose 11th-inning double in game six instantly became the 16-year-old team's most historic blow.

Thank you, Blue Jays, for bringing the 1992 World Series trophy to Canada.

CONTENTS

PART 5 — Diamond Dictators

PART 6 — Astounding Antics

FOREWORD

I WAS DELIGHTED when Brian McFarlane, who's known throughout most of North America for his hockey books and broadcasts, told me he was going to turn his literary attention to baseball's rich history. The result is *It Happened in Baseball,* one man's search through the record books, scrapbooks, and newspaper accounts of yesterday's diamond happenings, seeking fascinating facts and offbeat stories about what has become the North American pastime. This time the author's journey takes him around the bases instead of around a hockey rink. And just as he did with *It Happened in Hockey,* his recent bestseller about the winter game, he comes home a winner.

Arthur Daley, the famous American sportswriter, once wrote: "The baseball fan has the digestive apparatus of a billy goat. He can — and does — devour any set of diamond statistics with an insatiable appetite and then nuzzle hungrily for more. He'll swallow today's box scores and today's standings with one prodigious gulp. However, he is transformed into an epicure of the daintiest tastes imaginable the instant his daily fare is spiced with choice tidbits from the past. He savors every morsel and rolls his tongue appreciatively about each. He smacks his lips and drools with distressing impoliteness."

Daley said it well. And I, like you, am one of those billy goat fans. The grand old game of baseball provides a never-ending supply of unusual, bizarre, unbelievable events and moments that should be (and fortunately are) chronicled by competent writers. Fans of the game never tire of anecdotes involving the Babe, Dizzy, Casey, or Yogi. Many of modern-day baseball's personalities, men like Nolan Ryan, José Canseco, Kirby Puckett, Pete Rose, and the Toronto Blue Jays' own Dave Winfield, have made fascinating contributions to the lore of the game, dispelling the idea that baseball's past is far more exciting than its present.

Those of us who've been part of the Blue Jays family since day one will never forget the incredible debut of the Jays in the spring of 1977 when the home opener at old Exhibition Stadium was played in frigid temperatures during a snowstorm. More recently Blue Jay fans who turned out in 1992 to show their admiration and respect for the skills and leadership qualities of designated hitter Dave Winfield may recall how he was once castigated by many of the same fans when, as a visiting Yankee outfielder, he threw a ball that killed an innocent sea gull during a Jays game years ago. Both the Jays' snowy home opener in 1977 and Winfield's unintentional beaning of a sea gull drew enormous attention and have become a fascinating addition to the lore of the game.

In the brief history of the Blue Jays a handful of players could be singled out for inclusion in the pages ahead, some for their unique performances on the field, others for unusual escapades away from the SkyDome. There were the Jay sluggers who walloped a major league record 10 homers in a game against Baltimore (popular Ernie Whitt belted three of them), and there was Dave Stieb at the peak of his career, tossing three one-hitters in four starts. Then there was Glenallen Hill's awakening from a sound sleep in his apartment one night, terrified by a nightmare during which giant spiders were attacking him. In his bid to escape these crea-

A moment to savor! The 1992 Toronto Blue Jays celebrate in Atlanta after becoming the first team from outside the United States to capture the World Series. (Canada Wide)

tures Hill leaped out of bed, crashed into some furniture, and was injured seriously enough to be placed on the disabled list. After each of these occurrences, I'm sure one of us associated with the ball club must have said, "Now there's one for the book." Brian has included the Hill anecdote in *It Happened in Baseball* (although Glenallen would probably prefer to forget it) and the story of the 10-homer game, as well.

In his research for this book the author has studied the newspaper accounts and interviewed people who share his love for baseball history. Despite his extensive hockey background, Brian is no stranger to baseball. Growing up in Ottawa, he was a big fan of the Class C Ottawa Nationals of the Border League (his favorite player was Doug Harvey, a two-sport star who spent most of his winters guiding the Montreal Canadiens to one Stanley Cup after another). Later Brian was a fan of the Ottawa Athletics of the International League.

As a player, he describes himself as a "poor field, poor hit" type who always seemed to wind up as an infielder on a last-place team. One year in Ottawa his team in the Ottawa Senior League lost 23 games in a 24-game schedule. Late in the season he volunteered to pitch when his team's starter failed to show up. He amazed his mates — and himself, no doubt — by tossing a four-hitter and winning his team's only game of the season.

In 1951 he was offered a scholarship to St. Lawrence University in Canton, New York — not for his baseball talents but for his hockey ability — and there, for the local radio station, he did the play-by-play of the school's baseball games. One of the best of the varsity players of that era was pitcher Bob Shaw, who went on to major league stardom with the Chicago White Sox and other clubs.

When Brian started out in television in Schenectady, New York, his first guest on his very first telecast was Dodger hurler Johnny Podres who, two days earlier, had won the deciding game of the 1955 World Series. Brian says a pleasant part of his duties as a fledgling sportscaster in Schenectady was covering games played by the Eastern League Blue Jays.

Brian moved back to Canada in 1959, and in the early 1960s he and Tim Tyan served as the play-by-play voices of the baseball Maple Leafs on television. He recalls one afternoon when the action on the field was hot but the stadium roof they were broadcasting from was hotter. A fire broke out somewhere under the roof. The two nervous announcers could hear the wail of sirens in the distance as fire rigs raced to the old ballpark. They were tempted to evacuate the broadcast booth, but they gamely carried on, anxiously looking behind themselves after every pitch, expecting to see flames bursting through the roof at any moment. They called the game to the last pitch. Then they bolted for the stairwell leading to the stands below and safety. By then, unknown to them, the blaze had been extinguished, and they realized they'd been in no grave danger, after all.

That's hardly a story for *It Happened in Baseball*. But there are plenty of other strange and interesting ones in the pages ahead, even one about a memorable baseball event at Brian's alma mater, St. Lawrence University.

PAUL BEESTON
President, Toronto Blue Jays

ACKNOWLEDGMENTS

I AM INDEBTED to William Humber, chairman of Continuing Education at Seneca College in North York and author of two outstanding baseball books (*Let's Play Ball* and *Cheering for the Home Team: The Story of Baseball in Canada*), for his contributions. *The Baseball Encyclopedia* (New York: Macmillan, 1982) also proved helpful when it came to checking statistics. And, finally, special thanks to Janet Money, Linda Woodcock, Michael Carroll, senior editor at Stoddart Publishing, and to the helpful members of the North York Central Library staff.

PART

PEERLESS PLAYERS

Ty Cobb's Sorry Demise

HE WAS THE GEORGIA PEACH, the greatest player of his era. His lifetime average was .367 and he won 12 batting crowns. He collected 4,191 hits, scored 2,244 runs, and stole 892 bases. Old-timers say he won games single-handedly. Not surprisingly, he was the first player named to baseball's Hall of Fame.

Tyrus Raymond Cobb came from good stock. His father was a Georgia state senator, a man Ty worshipped. But his father met an untimely end: he had his head blown off by Ty's mother when Ty was just 18. His jealous father, suspecting his wife of infidelity, sneaked home from a trip one night and crept into his wife's bedroom. When she saw a dark figure enter the room, she snatched up a shotgun and blasted his head off. Some say this tragedy was largely responsible for Ty's belligerent behavior — on and off the playing field. Others say the vicious hazing he received from older teammates when he was a Detroit Tiger rookie warped his personality.

Few people could tolerate Ty. Most of his teammates hated him. One ball player, Elbie Felts, sued Cobb after being attacked by him. Fans heckled him and at least one was knocked unconscious by Cobb's flashing fists. Despite the fact that he was a millionaire many times over, no one would stay with him. Two wives, mistresses, servants — they all departed. Stories circulated about him assaulting one of his ex-wives, and on another occasion he allegedly struck a female member of his family across the nose with a baseball bat.

In the last year of his life he told his biographer Al Stump that he had killed a man in 1912. He said two hoodlums mugged him in Detroit. When one of the thugs knifed him in the back, Cobb pulled a gun and chased his attackers, pistol-whipping one to death when he caught up to him in a dark alley. He said he would have shot the man, but his gun jammed.

"Then, instead of seeking treatment for his wound," Stump relates, "Cobb went and played a ball game while wearing a blood-soaked bandage wrapped around his midsection. Got a double and a triple for Detroit. Only then did he get the wound in his back treated and stitched up. He was that kind of player through 3,033 games."

Cobb had a well-deserved reputation as a tight-wad. When fans sent him letters, he used the return-mail stamps for his own correspondence. But he had a generous side, too. He sent money to indigent ball players and financed the Cobb Educational Foundation, which helped hundreds of young men to get through college.

Wherever he went, Cobb carried an old brown bag containing more than $1 million in negotiable bonds and stock certificates. He also carried a loaded Luger, which he didn't hesitate to brandish whenever he was involved in a confrontation.

In his declining years, when ordered by doctors to stick to a strict diet (he had diabetes) and stay off booze, he refused to eat and went from a pint of whiskey a day to more than a quart. When he was hospitalized, his nurses never seemed able to find the bottles he hid in his room. They didn't realize the innocent-looking glass of liquid on the tray by his bed was pure vodka or gin — because his false teeth were in it.

Just before he died in an Atlanta hospital in

mid-July 1961 he wondered aloud if anyone would remember him. How could anyone who ever saw him play, or anyone who came in contact with his darker side, ever forget him?

Casey Stengel once said of Cobb, "I never saw anyone like him. No one even close to Cobb. When he wiggled those wild eyes at a pitcher, you knew you were looking at a bird nobody could beat. It was like he was superhuman."

Baseball's Napoleon and the Georgia Peach

NAPOLEON LAJOIE, a 200-pound six-footer, was one of the most graceful players who ever lived. And he was a marvel at the plate. Three times he led the American League in hitting, batting .422 one season and winding up a Hall of Fame career with a lifetime batting average of .339.

As the 1910 season reached its final weekend, tremendous interest was focused on the race for the batting title between Cleveland's Lajoie and fiery Ty Cobb of the Tigers. Cobb appeared to be a shoo-in and decided to rest on his laurels and sit out his team's last two games. Only a phenomenal performance by Lajoie in a season-ending double-header against the St. Louis Browns would enable him to wrest the batting crown away from Cobb.

The fans had no difficulty deciding who to root for. Lajoie was extremely popular; Cobb was not.

Before the first game of the twin bill, manager Jack "Peach Pie" O'Connor of the Browns told his third baseman, a rookie named John "Red" Corriden, to play Lajoie back on the grass.

"Back on the grass?" a disbelieving Corriden exclaimed. "Won't he bunt his way on if I'm back on the grass?"

"Just do as I say," the manager growled.

In his first time at bat Lajoie tripled. Then he took advantage of Corriden's deep position by bunting and reaching first before Corriden could charge in and grab the ball. He did it again in his next at-bat and twice more before the game ended. Nap was a perfect four for four at the plate in game one.

In the second game Nap singled in his first appearance and then cracked a vicious grounder at shortstop Bobby Wallace, who knocked the ball down but hurried the throw to first and was wide of the mark. It could easily have been scored a hit, but the official scorer charged Wallace with an error.

In his next three appearances Lajoie went back to bunting and dropped three down the third-base line for hits. His eight base hits for the day brought his average up to .3841. Despite his incredible finish, though, Lajoie couldn't quite overtake Cobb, whose average was .3848. The difference was seven ten-thousandths of a percentage point.

Nap's fans blamed the official scorer for the loss of the title, the man who stubbornly refused to credit Lajoie with a base hit on the grounder to Wallace. But American League president Ban Johnson's wrath was directed elsewhere. He was furious with Browns manager Jack O'Connor and scout Harry Howell.

"By ordering young Corriden to play back on the grass O'Connor was inviting Lajoie to help himself to some gift hits by way of bunts," Johnson insisted. "And Howell, I understand, made repeated trips to the press box to make sure those bunts were scored as hits. Their actions will not be tolerated."

On Johnson's insistence O'Connor and Howell were fired by Bob Hedges, the Browns' owner. Ironically Howell returned to the game as a minor league umpire, while O'Connor successfully sued for the remaining $5,000 on his contract but never participated in baseball again.

As for Lajoie, if he received half a dozen gift hits that day, which he undoubtedly did, those were the only ones he got among the 3,251 he collected during his illustrious career. And even if he didn't win the batting crown, he *was* awarded a brand-new Chalmers automobile along with Cobb.

Heartbreak for Haddix

ON MAY 26, 1959, Harvey Haddix, a Pittsburgh Pirate left-hander, tossed a perfect game for nine innings on the road against the Milwaukee Braves. His feat should have put him in select company, for only a handful of hurlers had ever pitched perfect games and all, as one might expect, emerged as winners.

But not Haddix. At the end of his flawless nine-inning performance the game was scoreless. He would have to carry on through extra innings. In the 10th, 11th, and 12th he put the Braves away easily, but still his teammates failed to produce the single run that would have made their popular little starter an instant hero.

Haddix began to weaken in the unlucky 13th. One Brave, Felix Mantilla, reached base when the Pirates' third baseman, Don Hoak, made a throwing error on an easy ground ball. Milwaukee slugger Eddie Mathews bunted down the line, sacrificing Mantilla to second. Haddix passed Hank Aaron intentionally to set up a possible double play for Joe Adcock, the next batter. But the strategy backfired when Adcock belted a three-run homer.

Even so, through a bizarre set of circumstances, Haddix almost got out of the inning unscathed. When Adcock homered, Mantilla raced for home. Aaron, on first, lost sight of Adcock's blow and thought the ball had remained in play. He assumed that Mantilla's run had ended the ball game, so he stopped halfway around the bases and headed for the Braves' dugout. Adcock, running out his homer, passed Aaron on the base paths and was called out. Aaron, too, might have been called out for illegal base running if Mantilla hadn't already crossed home plate. No run would have scored, and Haddix's quest for a perfect performance would have continued.

But Mantilla did cross home, split seconds before the mix-up on the base paths, and the Braves squeezed out a 1–0 victory.

Williams Tops .400

IN 1941 BOSTON RED SOX SLUGGER Ted Williams drilled so many shots to right field that Cleveland Indian manager Lou Boudreau invented the Williams Shift, loading up the right side of the diamond with fielders in an effort to cut down on the great hitter's safeties. Did Williams take advantage of the wide-open spaces Boudreau offered him on the left side? No, sir. He was too stubborn for that. "I hit to right because that's where my power is," he told reporters. "A couple of extra players over there won't stop me."

Williams might have hit .800 against Cleveland if he'd dropped hits to left and made Boudreau look foolish. But nobody argued with the man they called the Splendid Splinter, one of the most astute students of batting technique the game has ever produced.

It wasn't as though he couldn't hit to left. Manager Joe Cronin recalled the day Williams had jogged in from left field, red in the face. "There's a loudmouth fan sitting behind third base," Williams had growled, "and he's been riding me all game. Watch him jump for his life the next time I'm at bat. I'll put one right down his throat."

From the batter's box Williams sent foul after foul darting over third base, scattering the fans. "I kept count," Cronin said later. "Ted hit seventeen fouls over there, and the big-mouth he was trying to hit ducked on every one of them. Ted was never more than six feet off target."

Ted Williams, the Splendid Splinter, hit .406 in 1941, collecting six hits in eight trips to the plate in a season-ending doubleheader. (National Baseball Library)

9

"All I want out of life," Williams once said, "is that when I walk down the street folks will turn and say, 'There goes the greatest hitter who ever lived.'"

His best season ever was 1941. In September, with the year winding down, he was hitting at an unheard of .420 clip. But in the final few days of the season his batting average slipped until it was down to .3999. In baseball it would go into the record books as an even .400.

Prior to Boston's season-ending doubleheader, manager Cronin patted Williams on the shoulder. "Better sit out the final two games, kid. Nobody hits .400 anymore. It's a mark that may stand for years. Don't risk losing it."

Williams gave his manager a withering look. "If I'm gonna be a champion, I want to win like a champion," he insisted. "Besides, to me, hitting .399 isn't quite the same as .400."

That afternoon he went out and collected six hits in eight trips to the plate for a final average of .406. It's a mark that hasn't been equaled in over half a century.

Talk About Brotherly Love

IN THE THIRTIES THE GAS HOUSE GANG was the talk of baseball. Nobody seems to know who tagged the St. Louis Cardinals with the colorful nickname, but it suited them. They were unsophisticated roughnecks, most of them right off the farm, who would do anything to win. They fought opposing teams tooth-and-nail and they fought each other, too. Outfielder Joe Medwick once knocked pitcher Ed Heuser unconscious midway through a game because the hurler accused him of not hustling. Kayoed him right in the dugout. Medwick also flattened another teammate, pitcher Tex Carleton, outside the batting cage before a game. Carleton, it seems, was tardy in leaving the cage to give Medwick his batting practice turn, which steamed the veteran.

Star pitcher Dizzy Dean once accused Medwick of loafing during a game. Medwick snarled at him, "You worry about the pitching, big-mouth, and I'll take care of the outfield."

Dean, who was at the end of the dugout, snarled back, "I'm coming down there and give you a good punch in the mouth."

Dean started toward Medwick, and his brother Paul got up and joined him. The Dean brothers were close. If one was going to fight, the other would be right beside him. They didn't frighten Medwick. He brandished a bat and said, "Let's see if the wood in this bat matches the wood in your heads."

All of the Cardinals jumped in and kept them apart. An inning or two later Medwick hit a mammoth home run. When he came back to the dugout, he took a long drink of water, then spat it all over Dizzy's shoes. "Now let's see you hold the lead I've given you, you gutless so-and-so," he growled out of the corner of his mouth.

The Dean brothers leaped at Medwick. Once again quick action by the other Cardinals kept them from grabbing the outfielder by the throat.

That was in 1934, the season Dizzy Dean was a holdout in training camp. He wasn't holding out for himself but for his brother Paul. Dizzy signed for close to $8,000 while Paul, a rookie who had never pitched a game in the majors, signed for $3,000.

"You took advantage of the kid," Dizzy screamed. "He's worth a lot more than $3,000, and I'm not playing until he gets more dough." So Dean was a holdout while Paul, eager to get a chance to play, dutifully worked out every day. The team finally chipped in a few more dollars for Paul, and when everything was straightened out, the brothers talked to the press.

"How many games will you and your brother win this year?" Dizzy was asked.

"I figure 45," Dizzy replied.

"But your kid brother's never pitched in the majors."

"Don't matter. He's good. Nearly as good as I am, and I won 20 last year."

The reporters went away laughing. So did the Cardinals who had been eavesdropping on their boastful teammate.

But the Dean brothers had the last laugh. Dizzy won 30 that year and Paul won 19. And in the World Series they each won two games against the Detroit Tigers, with Dizzy tossing a shutout at the Tigers in the seventh game. You could, as they say, look it up.

A Surprise Party for DiMaggio

FOR THREE MONTHS IN 1941 baseball fans everywhere followed the amazing hitting streak fashioned by Joltin' Joe DiMaggio. It began innocently enough on May 15 when the Yankee Clipper slapped out a single in a game against the Chicago White Sox. That unremarkable

After hitting safely in 56 consecutive games, Joe DiMaggio embarked on another hitting streak of 16 games. (National Baseball Library)

hit was the beginning of the longest hitting streak in baseball history, one that may never be matched.

DiMaggio hit safely in the next game and the one after that. He crushed the ball in 10, 20, 30 straight games. In midsummer he passed the previous consecutive game hit record of 44 games, set back in 1898 by Wee Willie Keeler.

There were at least three close calls as the streak continued. One afternoon, playing against the St. Louis Browns, DiMaggio went into the ninth inning of a game without a safety. Eldon Auker, the Browns' submariner, had muffled DiMaggio's bat in all of his previous trips to the plate. In the ninth there was a chance Auker would escape another confrontation, for DiMaggio was the fourth man due up. But a Yankee reached first and Joe stepped in. He rifled Auker's first pitch into center field for a double.

In another game against the Philadelphia Athletics, A's pitcher John Babich decided to walk DiMaggio every time he faced him. In the Yankee Clipper's first at-bat Babich threw four balls wide of the plate and the Yankee star strolled to first.

In his second at-bat DiMaggio fumed as Babich served three more balls well away from the strike zone. The fourth pitch was as bad as the rest, high and outside, but DiMaggio leaned out and smacked it. The ball zipped through the legs of the startled pitcher and the streak was still alive.

In the game in which he needed to produce a hit to break Keeler's 44-game record, DiMag faced the Red Sox. In two at-bats he hit a pair of tremendous drives to the outfield. Stan Spence hauled in one, and Joe's brother Dom caught the other. Joe's confidence plummeted, for Heber Newsome, the Red Sox starter, was at the top of his game, and Joe always had trouble hitting Newsome. In his next trip the Red Sox pitcher threw a fastball, and DiMag belted it out of the ballpark.

The streak ended finally in the 57th game against Cleveland. In that contest DiMaggio sent a couple of scorchers down the third-base line, but the Indians' Ken Keltner made two extraordinary plays.

"They were brazen robberies," DiMaggio told reporters after the game. "They were sure hits turned into outs because of Keltner's incredible performance."

Recalling that night half a century ago, Keltner said, "One ball he hit so hard and low and fast I thought it might get by me. But I made a backhand stab and got it in my glove. My momentum carried me a couple of strides across the foul line before I could stop, turn, and throw to first. I got him by an eyelash. Joe was the greatest player ever. He was so popular I needed a police escort to get to my car after the game. And this was in Cleveland! There were a lot of Italians living there and they loved Joe. They were furious with me for what I did to him. Joe still calls me the Culprit whenever we meet."

Another Cleveland player who must share the blame, or take credit, for ending the streak was

14

shortstop Lou Boudreau. Later in the game DiMaggio smashed one into the hole. The ball hit a pebble and changed direction, but Boudreau, with his marvelous quick hands, collared it and turned a double play. "It just wasn't my day," DiMaggio said. "The ball to Boudreau almost caught him in the ear. I don't know how he got his glove on it. But the streak had to end sometime."

Following the game that ended the most amazing streak in baseball history, DiMaggio was treated to a surprise party back at the team's hotel. All the Yankees, including manager Joe McCarthy, were there. The players presented Joe with a sterling silver humidor. Number 56 was inscribed on it as well as 91, commemorating the number of hits he'd compiled during the streak. "I've had a lot of thrills out of baseball," Joe later said. "But that gift from my teammates was the most beautiful thing I ever saw. And the reception they gave me was the thrill of a lifetime."

What did DiMaggio do for an encore? He started another streak — this one lasting for 16 games.

Baseball's Most Durable Pitcher

IN 1884 CHARLIE "OLD HOSS" RADBOURN set records for endurance that will never be matched. During the season, he pitched an astounding total of 678⅔ innings. He appeared in 73 games as a starter and reliever, winning 60, and on his days off he played the infield.

Teenager Radbourn joined the Providence Grays of the National League in 1880 after playing half a dozen games with Buffalo as an infielder during the previous season. Even though the 16-year-old had never pitched a major league game, he told Providence manager Frank Bancroft he thought he could do an adequate job as a hurler. Within two years Radbourn was one of the best pitchers in the game. In 1883 he pitched in 632 innings, appeared in 77 games, and finished with an awesome record of 49–25.

Radbourn was even better the following season, even though manager Bancroft had him sharing the work load with Charlie Sweeney, another top-notch hurler. But Sweeney proved to be a troublemaker. He was caught drinking between innings and began missing practices. Once he refused to leave the mound when Bancroft called for a relief pitcher, and after a bitter argument with the manager, he quit the team and jumped to an outlaw league.

That left the bulk of the pitching chores to Radbourn, who appeared in every game for the final two months of the season. In four of those games he played the infield. Old Hoss guided the Grays on a 20-game win streak and set a personal major league record by winning 18 games in a row. (In 1888 Tim Keefe would surpass the mark, winning 19 consecutive games, and in 1912 Rube Marquard tied Keefe's record, also winning 19 straight.)

But Radbourn's effectiveness in 1884 was truly phenomenal. After Sweeney quit the team, Hoss won 30 games, lost four, and tied one. And he did it with an arm that was so sore and overworked that he couldn't raise it to comb his hair in the morning. It took him hours to get ready for each day's game. He would appear at the ballpark long before starting time and begin tossing the ball a few feet. Gradually he would increase the distance until he could throw the ball from the outfield to home plate. When he gave a little nod, signaling that he was ready to play, his teammates would breathe a sigh of relief. They knew Old Hoss would be invincible in the nine innings that lay ahead.

When the pennant-winning Grays completed their season on October 15, Radbourn tossed an 8–0 shutout in the final game. He had accounted for 60 of his team's 84 wins and had completed all 74 of his starting assignments. His final mark was 60–12–2. He led the league in strikeouts with 441, and his sparkling 1.38 earned run average topped all other pitchers.

But Radbourn's mound chores weren't quite finished. Providence decided to challenge the New York Metropolitans, champions of the American Association, to a three-game series for the "championship of baseball." It was a forerunner to the World Series.

Old Hoss limbered up his arm and tossed a 6–0 shutout in the opening game, played before a mere 2,500 fans. Inclement weather kept the crowd away for game two, and fewer than a thousand turned out to witness Radbourn win again by a 3–1 score. Only a few hundred showed up for game three as the series had already been decided. Only after Radbourn won again — by a 12–2 count — could he rest his weary arm.

Even though Radbourn pitched well over the next half-dozen years, he never again came close to matching his miracle season of 1884. He finished his remarkable career with 311 victories, good enough to earn him a place in the Hall of Fame.

Iron Man Joe McGinnity

PERHAPS HE WAS CALLED IRON MAN because he once worked in a foundry. More likely he earned the nickname because of his willingness to work hard, and often, as a major league pitcher. Joe McGinnity, baseball's Iron Man, pitched in the majors from 1899 to 1908 — he didn't break in until he was 28 — and still holds records that may never be broken.

For example:

- McGinnity started 391 games and completed 314 of them.
- He pitched both ends of a doubleheader five times in his career.
- In one season he won both ends of a doubleheader three times.
- He won five games in six days while with the Dodgers and 10 games in 12 days with the Giants.

Among his other feats:

- In 1903 he started 48 games and completed 44 of them.
- He won 247 games, an average of almost 25 per season.
- He averaged 345 innings per season and ended his 10-year career with a winning percentage of .632, one of the highest such marks ever recorded.

He was a tough competitor and mean. He once welcomed a new umpire to the league by spitting in his face. After his major league career, he toiled in the minors for several years, racking up 171 wins and hurling his final game at age 54.

Teenage Phenom

MODERN-DAY BALL PLAYERS usually require some seasoning in the minors. Very few ever become big league regulars before the age of 20. But before the turn of the century teenage phenoms were common in baseball, and one of them was pitcher Monte Ward.

In 1878 Ward, then 18, joined the Providence club and proved to be a sensation, winning 22 games. The following year, at 19, he compiled the astonishing total of 47 wins, a record number of victories in a single season for any teenage hurler.

Over the next three seasons Ward added another 77 wins to his total, but by then his frequent assignments had played havoc with his arm and he was forced to give up pitching. However, he didn't leave the game. He resumed his career as a better-than-average infielder and played another 10 seasons, finishing his 17-year career with a .275 batting average.

The Almost .400 Hitter

EVEN THOUGH HE WAS MAKING A MILLION dollars a year in 1980, third baseman George Brett of the Kansas City Royals was eager to sign an off-season contract for $250 a day — as a hockey player.

When a movie production company was filming

the story of the U.S. hockey team's dramatic gold medal victory in the 1980 Olympics, Brett went to the Los Angeles Sports Arena and wangled a part in the movie — as a Finnish player named Leinonon. Brett, a fair skater and puckhandler in his youth, was seen losing a face-off. That was it. In less than 10 seconds his movie career was over.

If Brett's skating and acting skills are less than memorable, his accomplishments at the plate in 1980 were awesome. Early in the season he was hitting a mere .247. By the All-Star break his average had jumped to .337, and by the end of the season he was a bona fide threat to become the first .400 hitter since Ted Williams hit .406 in 1941. Millions of fans followed the daily box scores and Brett's assault on the magic number, and most were disappointed when he fell short by five hits and finished with a .390 average. One additional hit would have put him ahead of legendary John McGraw, who batted .391 in 1899, the best average for a third baseman in history.

What can't be forgotten is that Brett's average soared despite a number of injuries. He missed nine games with a bruised heel, 26 with torn ligaments in his right ankle, and nine in September with a bruised hand. What troubled him even more all season was an embarrassing case of hemorrhoids, an ailment that required surgery in the middle of the World Series between the Royals and the Phillies. "It hurt so much," Brett says, "that I actually prayed Hal McRae would strike out in game two. I was on first base and couldn't bear the thought of running the bases if Hal connected." After surgery he met the press and said, "My problems are all behind me now."

Mickey Mantle Stays On

IN 1966 MICKEY MANTLE, the great New York Yankee switch-hitter, was contemplating retirement. In the previous season his RBI total had dipped to 56, but his .288 batting average was still impressive and he'd belted 28 home runs.

However, his friends, and Yankee management, urged him to stay on. "Look, you're just four home runs away from 500," they said. "And you have a chance to overtake Boston's Ted Williams, who retired with 521 homers. Why not hang in for another year or two, Mick?"

So Mantle came back in 1967 and chalked up 22 homers for a career total of 518, just three shy of Williams's mark and only 16 behind Jimmy Foxx's 534. Again he thought it was time to bow out.

"But, Mick," his pals said, "you're a cinch to pass Foxx if you play one more season. Don't quit just yet."

So, in 1968, Mantle was back in a Yankee uniform, swatting homers and trying to keep his batting average up. He clouted enough homers — 18 — to pass Foxx on the all-time homer list, finishing with a lifetime 536.

And that was enough. The slugger ahead of him on the home run list was Willie Mays, whose total of 660 was pretty much out of sight. So Mantle finally retired.

While the extra two seasons he put in enabled him to jump ahead of Williams and Foxx in the home run derby, his batting average slipped dramatically, plummeting to .245 and .237. By playing the additional two seasons, Mantle's lifetime average dropped under .300.

There are only three members of the select 3,000 hit club in major league baseball who failed to end their careers with a .300 average or better. Mantle is one of them. The others are Carl Yastrzemski and Lou Brock.

Old Aches and Pains

WHEN HE DIED IN ATLANTA early in January 1991 at the age of 83, Luke Appling left behind a number of impressive baseball accomplishments — more than enough to earn him a place in the Hall of Fame. In 1936, the finest of his 20 seasons playing shortstop for the Chicago White Sox, he batted .388 and drove in 128 runs. No other shortstop has ever approached that average, which was good enough that year to lead the American League. Nor has a shortstop ever played as many seasons as Appling, known as Old Aches and Pains, a nickname he earned by consistently complaining about how terrible he felt, often before going out to play a sensational game.

His career batting average over 21 seasons was .310, and in 1970 he was named the greatest player in White Sox history. But when asked about his biggest thrill in baseball, he named a moment that took place long after his major league career was over.

In the summer of 1982, when Appling was 75 years old, he was asked to play in an Old-timers' game at RFK Stadium. He led off the first inning of the game, facing another Hall of Famer, pitcher Warren Spahn, who served up a pitch that Appling hammered deep into the left-field stands, a dozen rows back. It was an astonishing feat. Nobody could recall anyone of Appling's advanced age belting a ball out of a major league park.

Old Aches and Pains made the most of his big moment. He scampered around the bases as Spahn chased and swatted him in mock anger across the backside with his glove. When he reached home plate, Appling staggered, held a hand to his chest, and feigned a heart attack. Then he doffed his cap to the crowd, which was on its feet, grinned, and entered the dugout.

He would say later, "I got more reaction from fans around the country from that one swing than I did in 21 big league seasons. It was wonderful."

The Babe's First Pro Dinger

WHO SAYS TORONTO HASN'T GOT a long tradition when it comes to baseball? It may have taken until 1992 for the city to win the World Series, but back on September 5, 1914, Toronto witnessed George Herman Ruth's very first professional home run, his sole four-bagger in his brief stint in the minors.

The place: Toronto Maple Leafs' baseball park at Hanlan's Point on the Island. The occasion: the first game of a doubleheader between the Leafs and Ruth's International League Providence Grays.

The war in Europe had been raging for a month, and no doubt the citizens of Toronto had more on their minds than the auspicious event that occurred that Saturday morning. As the *Toronto Daily Star* described it, "'Babe' Ruth, the Grays' youthful southside phenom, held the Leafs to a single clout in the fourth, and had them all smothered on the nigh side of second base, hence the 9–0 stuff."

Besides getting a one-hit shutout, the 19-year-old Sultan of Swat also got, the newspaper noted in passing, a home run, one of 15 hits the Grays stroked off Leaf pitcher Ellis Johnson. What the paper doesn't say is that it was a three-run homer that sailed over the right-field fence. Later legend would attest that the dinger had soared into Lake Ontario. And some would even swear that the ball had last been seen on its way to the United States.

But the Babe wasn't finished with Toronto yet. In August 1923 he returned with the mighty Yankees for an exhibition game with the hometown Maple Leafs. This time Ruth really did hammer the ball over the bleachers and into the lake, but the Yankees, no doubt clowning around, lost the game 8–2.

That year Babe Ruth crunched 41 homers, leading the American League once again. All told he bagged 12 home run crowns, more than any other major leaguer. And to think that it all began in Toronto the Good.

Now Pitching for the Red Sox — Ted Williams

IN LATE AUGUST 1940, before America's entrance into the Second World War reduced all major league rosters to a cast of veterans and minor league suspects, Boston manager Joe Cronin did his best to put a surprise in the record books.

Trailing the Tigers 11–1 in the first game of a doubleheader, he called in left fielder Ted Williams to pitch the eighth inning. Williams finished the game, giving up three hits but striking out Rudy York.

Williams is perhaps the greatest hitter the game ever saw. He recorded the last .400 season in the big leagues one year later and ended his career in dramatic fashion by hitting a home run in his final major league at-bat in 1960. And while pitching appearances such as his are unusual, they occur often enough to produce some interesting results.

In 1968 slugger Rocky Colavito pitched two and two-thirds innings of scoreless ball for the Yankees and actually scored the winning run to give himself the pitching victory. In June 1978 the expansion Blue Jays pounded Baltimore 24–10, and among their mound victims was Oriole outfielder Larry Harlow, who gave up five runs. Catcher Elrod Hendricks, however, surrendered only one hit in his two-and-one-third-inning appearance.

Less surprising was the complete game pitching performance of Babe Ruth in the final game of the 1933 season. Ruth began his career as a very successful pitcher with the Boston Red Sox, and only his superior talent as a home run hitter led him to an everyday position in the lineup as a left fielder.

With the pennant already decided in Washington's favor, the Yanks started Ruth in the hope of drawing a curious crowd. Over 25,000 attended and, but for a sixth-inning uprising when Boston scored four, Ruth was always in command, winning in his last ever major league pitching appearance. In the process he belted his 34th homer of the season from his usual third spot in the batting order.

Catcher Joe Glenn recalled that the 38-year-old

Ruth still had average pitcher's speed on his fastball and kept batters confused with a mixture of curves, change-ups, and good location.

Two Yanks in Home Run Battle

IT IS ALWAYS EXCITING when two great players go head-to-head in the battle for the home run championship. In the fall of 1931 a crazy mix-up cost New York Yankee Lou Gehrig the title.

Gehrig and Babe Ruth were neck-and-neck in the home run derby when the Yanks played host to the Washington Senators. For some obscure reason Yankee manager Joe McCarthy decided to take over as third-base coach for the afternoon. With two out and Lyn Lary on first, Gehrig stepped up to the plate and smashed a drive toward the right-field stands.

As Lary rounded second base, he glanced up and saw one of the Washington outfielders with the ball in his glove. Not realizing that the ball had bounced

Lou Gehrig (left) and Babe Ruth. Ruth's final home run, his 714th, was one of the longest he ever hit. Gehrig set a major league record by playing in 2,130 consecutive games. (National Baseball Library)

out of the stands and back onto the field where the outfielder had grabbed it, Lary crossed the third-base line and headed straight for the dugout. He believed that Gehrig's blast had been caught for the third out.

Meanwhile Gehrig happily rounded the bases and reached home, unaware that Lary hadn't scored ahead of him. Gehrig was stunned when the umpire called him out for passing a base runner.

But Lary wasn't the only Yankee asleep at the switch on Gehrig's homer. Manager McCarthy had to share the blame for the embarrassing mix-up. It was his job, as third-base coach, to guide the base runners home. But when the ball cleared the fence, McCarthy ignored the runners, his first priority, and began jumping up and down with his back to the field, celebrating Gehrig's homer.

Instead of a homer Gehrig was awarded a triple. He and Ruth finished the season tied for the home run title — each with 46. As for manager McCarthy, he stayed in the dugout for the rest of the season.

The Author Returns

IN THE 1960s JIM BOUTON of the Yankees was one of the most successful pitchers in baseball. He won 21 games for New York in 1963 and was named to the All-Star team. In 1964 he won 18 plus two World Series games against the St. Louis Cardinals and continued to throw hard until he injured his arm the following year. With some of the zip gone from his fastball, he was forced to develop a knuckler to stay in the league. He lasted until 1970 when he retired to write a book about his experiences in baseball.

The book — *Ball Four* — was a big success, and a shocker. Bouton told a few truths about baseball, about the sexual escapades and the drinking habits of the players. Players named in the book were furious, and most of the owners were, too. The commissioner tried, unsuccessfully, to have the book banned. But all this publicity helped make *Ball Four* a runaway bestseller and over 200,000 hardcover copies were sold.

Jim "Author" Bouton, however, became a baseball outcast, so unpopular that he wasn't even invited back to Yankee Stadium for Old-timers' Days. Journalists called him Judas and Benedict Arnold. Dick Young of the *New York News* described him as a social leper.

When Bouton, at age 39, decided on a comeback in 1977, most doors were slammed in his face. Bill Veeck gave him a chance to pitch in Double A ball, but he was released after a few weeks. After that, Bouton says, "All 26 major league clubs refused to let me even try out for one of their 112 farm teams."

Then Bouton got lucky. He ran into Ted Turner, owner of the Atlanta Braves. Turner himself was 39 and was the employer of another 39-year-old — knuckleballer Hoyt Wilhelm. Turner said to Bouton, "Jim, I'll give you a chance to make one of our minor league teams. Report to our camp in Florida." Bouton did so and looked sharp in spring training. He pitched 13 scoreless innings. Then he was released. No reason given, just dismissed.

Angry as hell, he flew to Atlanta and met with Turner. He told the owner about the great training camp he'd had and the miserable treatment he'd received. Turner got on the phone and told general manager Bill Lucas to find a place for Bouton . . . or else. Forced to obey, Lucas assigned Bouton to the Braves' minor league team in Richmond — as the batting practice pitcher. For six weeks Bouton threw batting practice before each Richmond game. When the game began, he would shower, get dressed, and watch the other players perform.

Early in the season an exhibition game was arranged with the Atlanta Braves, and Ted Turner told the manager he wanted to see Bouton pitch. So the batting practice hurler started for Richmond, lasted seven innings, struck out seven of the Braves, and was leading 3–1 when he left to thunderous applause. Only then did Bill Lucas agree to let him pitch some real ball and dispatched him to Savannah of the Southern League.

In Savannah, playing for a last-place club, Bouton pitched a one-hitter, a two-hitter, and a 13-inning shutout. He became the first pitcher ever to win the league's hustlingest player award. Toward the end of the season the Atlanta Braves decided to call him up. Ten years after he first retired he was back in the Show. Within days he stopped the Giants 4–1, his first major league win since 1970.

Bouton hurled a few more games, but he felt there was something missing his second time around. He was uninterested and bored with life in the majors. He'd eaten in all the fancy restaurants and stayed in the four- and five-star hotels. He'd been on hundreds of flights to cities from coast-to-coast. He discovered he missed the long bus rides with his Savannah buddies, the broom-closet hotel rooms, and the bowls of chili in greasy spoons at 3:00 a.m.

So he thanked his friend Ted Turner for giving

him a second big league chance and told him he wouldn't be back the following season. He'd done what he'd set out to do, starting from scratch. It was time to leave. And with no regrets.

Roger Maris No Mere Asterisk

THROUGHOUT HIS CAREER and the remainder of his life Roger Maris was dogged by the persistent claim that his 61 home runs in 1961 couldn't be compared with Ruth's 60 in 1927. Pundits pointed out that there were eight more games in the 1961 season as a result of the American League's expansion to 10 teams.

Commissioner Ford Frick even went so far as to have an asterisk placed in the baseball record book to indicate that Maris's 61 home runs were struck in a 162-game season. Babe's one-season record would only be broken, Frick said, if a player did it in 154 games or less. It was the final indignity for Maris, who endured the season-long stress of pursuing the record alongside popular Yankee teammate Mickey Mantle, the clear favorite of reporters and fans alike.

Maris hit number 59 in the third inning of the 154th game. He hit number 60 in the season's 159th game and belted his 61st homer in the fourth inning of the season finale against Red Sox rookie right-hander Tracy Stallard, smashing the ball into the lower right-field stands about 360 feet away. Over 25,000 Yankee Stadium fans gave him a five-minute standing ovation.

"Whether I beat Ruth's record or not is for others to say, but it gives me a wonderful feeling to know that I'm the only man in history to hit 61 home runs. Nobody can take that away from me," he said after the game.

Despite all the controversy, Maris did manage to beat Ruth in one other little-known statistic. The Babe had taken 689 plate appearances to reach 60 while Maris connected in his 684th trip to the plate. "I'm not saying I'm of the Babe's caliber," Maris offered, "but I'm glad to say I hit more than he did in a season."

Ironically another of the Bambino's records tumbled in that fall's World Series with hardly any fuss at all. Yankee pitcher Whitey Ford completed 32 scoreless World Series innings stretching back to his shutouts in the 1960 series. The old mark of 29⅔ innings was set by Ruth as a pitcher for the Boston Red Sox during the 1916 and 1918 fall classics.

Those Amazing Old-timers

EVENTUALLY FATHER TIME CATCHES UP to all ball players, but some big leaguers were able to avoid the old fellow's clutches until they were well past middle age.

Two pitchers hold the distinction of being the oldest "regulars" on big league rosters. Knuckleballer Hoyt Wilhelm, after 21 years with eight different clubs, was just five days short of his 49th birthday when he was released by the Dodgers in 1973. Jack Quinn, whose spitballs baffled batters for 23 seasons, was 50 years old when he retired from the game. Quinn is the only pitcher to win a game at age 49, and the only hurler to lose one at that advanced age.

Leroy "Satchel" Paige tossed three scoreless innings against the Boston Red Sox at age 59.

(National Baseball Library)

Quinn, however, wasn't the oldest pitcher to appear in a big league game. In 1965, as a publicity stunt, 59-year-old Satchel Paige became the oldest player in history when he tossed three scoreless innings for the Kansas City Athletics against the Boston Red Sox. Old Satch had been out of baseball for 12 years when he was reactivated. He gave up one hit during his stint — to Carl Yastrzemski, holder of the American League's best slugging percentage that season.

In that game Paige surpassed the record of Nick Altrock who, at age 57, took part in a game as a pinch hitter in 1933. Because Altrock didn't get a hit in the contest, Minnie Minoso of the White Sox, at age 53, has the distinction of being the oldest player to hit safely in a game.

The Bambino Bows Out

EARLY IN THE 1935 SEASON virtually no one expected anything from Babe Ruth. Overweight, 40 years old, and beset with personal problems, the legendary Yankee slugger was little more than a curiosity piece when he was traded to the Boston Braves, the only team that would take him. By mid-May of that year the man who had hit 60 homers in 1927 was an easy out almost every time he hobbled to the plate. For the first time in his career his batting average slipped below .200.

Then on May 25, a Sunday afternoon, the aging Bambino took the field against the Pirates in Pittsburgh. On his first trip to the plate he hit a long home run into the right-field stands. A couple of innings later he sent another fastball soaring into the bleachers. The next time up Ruth banged out a single that scored a run.

By the time the Babe stepped up to the plate again late in the game, the fans were clamoring for another home run. The old man quickly obliged. He brought the crowd to its feet with a towering blast to right that sailed clear out of Forbes Field. No one in the long history of Pittsburgh baseball had ever hit a ball over those right-field stands.

As Ruth rounded the bases, few could guess that this awesome home run, number 714 of the Babe's illustrious career, would be his last. A week later he announced his retirement. Who would argue that the three home runs he hit that day were a fitting finale to a career like no other in baseball?

PART

GLORIOUS GAMES

The Pawtucket Marathon

BACK IN 1920 THE BOSTON BRAVES and the Brooklyn Dodgers sent Joe Oeschger and Leon Cadore to the mound to pitch for their respective teams. Twenty-six innings and just three hits later the umpire called the game a no-decision.

Was it the longest game in professional baseball history? It was until April 19, 1981, 61 years later, when the Pawtucket Red Sox and the Rochester Red Wings, two International League rivals, headed into the top of the 33rd inning tied at two. That was when league president Harold Cooper stepped in and suspended the game, stating it would be completed at a later date.

On June 23 of the same year, with major league baseball players on strike, attention was focused on McCoy Stadium in Pawtucket, Rhode Island, for the 33rd inning (and resumption) of the longest game ever played. Bob Ojeda, the starting pitcher for Pawtucket, gave up a one-out single to Cal Ripken, Jr., before retiring the side. In the bottom half of the inning Rochester starter Steve Grilli got into trouble early when he hit Marty Barrett with the first pitch. Chico Walker singled and Grilli walked the next batter to load the bases.

Cliff Speck came in to relieve Grilli, and the fans got to their feet as Dave Korza stepped up to the plate. Korza worked the count to two balls and two strikes before ripping the fifth pitch into left field, bringing home Barrett with the winning run.

The entire game lasted eight hours and 43 minutes while the 33rd inning took only 18 minutes to play. The marathon set numerous records, including most at-bats (212), most strikeouts (59), and most baseballs required (156).

Reporters came from all over North America to cover the unique event. There were even two Japanese reporters in attendance from Tokyo's *Manachi Daily News.*

A Tripleheader Ended Their Season

THE BASEBALL DOUBLEHEADER is quickly going the way of tobacco-chewing catchers. Today's doubleheaders are usually played to make up for games lost because of rain-outs, riots, or other calamities.

But on the last weekend of the 1920 season Cincinnati and Pittsburgh were battling for third place in the National League. The Pirates trailed the Reds by 3½, but victories in their three remaining games over Cincinnati would earn them a small financial reward. Rain dashed Friday's game. With a doubleheader already scheduled for Saturday and both teams playing other rivals on Sunday, it looked as if the standings were secure for Cincinnati.

However, the Pirates' owner, Barney Dreyfuss, came up with a bright idea. He contacted National League president John Heydler and proposed that rarest of all baseball attractions — the tripleheader. Heydler told him to go ahead. On Saturday, October 2, the two teams took to the field at noon. As defending World Series champs (in the infamous 1919 Black Sox series), the Reds could hardly be excited by such a long day's schedule. Perhaps angered by the Pirates' refusal to give up on their dream of third, Cincinnati scored eight early runs and went on to win the opener 13–4.

With third place secure but two more games to play that day, Reds manager Pat Moran sat out his regulars and started four pitchers. Buck Benton was on the hill, Dutch Ruether at first, Fritz Coumbe in center, and Rube Bressler in right. Even so the Reds won again. By now darkness was approaching, but on to the third game they went. Finally the third game was called after six innings with the Pirates up 6–0.

Three games in one day had been played before, but they'd been split between separate admissions for a single morning game and an afternoon twin bill. Only in Pittsburgh did fans get three contests for the price of one.

Baseball's Craziest Doubleheader

THE LONGEST DAY OF THE YEAR came three weeks early for New York Met fans as a 1964 Sunday doubleheader dragged on for 10 hours and 16 minutes. Few of the original 57,037 fans were left when the San Francisco Giants finally pushed across two runs in the top of the 23rd inning of the second game. The Giants had won a more orderly first game 5–3.

The second game was reported in millions of American living rooms when Ed Sullivan brought viewers of his live Sunday evening show up-to-date on its progress. There were later reports of a fan catching a flight to the coast after the first game and arriving in his hotel room in San Francisco in time to catch the last few innings of the second game.

The 32 innings of baseball surpassed the 29 played by Boston and Philadelphia in an American League game in 1905. Among the highlights of this long day's journey into night was a Met triple play in the 14th inning. A Jésus Alou single and a Willie Mays walk brought Orlando Cepeda to the plate. He had gone 6 for 10 that afternoon, but this time he lined out to shortstop Roy McMillan, who stepped on second to retire Alou and then threw to Ed Kranepool at first, catching Mays off base.

The victory went to future Hall of Famer Gaylord Perry, who pitched 10 innings from the 13th through the 22nd before coming out for pinch hitter Del Crandall, who drove in the winning run on a two-out ground rule double to right field. Perry later said that it was the first game in which he threw a spitball. Losing pitcher Galen Cisco had pitched eight scoreless innings of relief before succumbing in the 23rd. In those days Met pitchers came to expect such fates.

Ironically the first game was also won by a future Hall of Famer — Juan Marichal. By the end of the second game, however, few remembered.

Hitless Wonders in Stunning Series Upset

THE INITIAL UPSET IN WORLD SERIES play took place in the first Series in 1903 when the Boston Pilgrims (four years later they would become the Red Sox) surprised powerful Pittsburgh by winning the best-of-nine confrontation five games to three. An oddity of the first Series ever played was that it produced two three-game winners: Boston's Bill Dineen and Pittsburgh's Deacon Phillippe. The latter won three, lost two, and worked all 44 innings of the five games.

But a much bigger upset took place in 1906 in an all-Chicago Series between the White Sox and the Cubs. The Cubs finished the season with a record 116 wins. This was the team of Joe Tinker, Johnny Evers, and player-manager Frank Chance. Pitchers included Mordecai "Three Finger" Brown, Orval Overall, and Ed Reulbach. The Cubs had won 50 of their final 58 games, and a sweep of their lightly regarded crosstown rivals appeared to be almost a certainty.

The White Sox, with a team batting average of .230, lowest in the American League, were known as the Hitless Wonders. Most people were amazed that a team with such a puny batting average had been able to reach the Series in the first place.

It was pitching that had carried the White Sox all season and won them a Series berth. And it was pitching that carried them to one of the great upsets in series history. Spitballer Ed Walsh won two games, Nick Altrock and Doc White one apiece. The batting star turned out to be George Rohe, a utility man who couldn't crack the infield of the Hitless Wonders until the shortstop was injured. Rohe batted .333, his seven hits including two triples and a double.

Merkle Was No Bonehead

HOW WOULD YOU LIKE TO BE KNOWN as Bonehead throughout your life? This cruel nickname, given to ball player Fred Merkle when he was just a rookie with the New York Giants, was an unfair reflection on his intelligence and on his skills as a ball player.

It was a name he didn't deserve but one he was stuck with. Fred Merkle, a first baseman, joined the Giants in 1907 at the tender age of 18. A year later, as a seldom-used bench warmer, he was to receive more abuse and criticism than any ball player, teenager or otherwise, ever warranted.

The Giants were playing the Chicago Cubs at the Polo Grounds in New York on a September day in 1908. The two teams were in a neck-and-neck race for the pennant with only a couple of weeks left in the season. Fred Merkle was a substitute for the Giants' regular first baseman Fred Tenney.

It was a tradition in those days at the Polo Grounds for the fans to swarm onto the field after every ball game. They were eager to mingle with players and get their autographs. Many of them weren't shy about giving an umpire or a player a dressing-down if he'd had a bad day. As a result, immediately after each game, the Giants made a beeline for their clubhouse, which was located under the center-field bleachers, a 30-second sprint from their dugout. The players raced to the safety of their quarters right after the final out. It was habit, a standard practice.

The game reached the bottom of the ninth with the score tied 1–1. With two out and a Giant runner on first, Merkle came to bat and hit a single to right. That placed Giants on first and third with Al Bridwell coming to the plate. Bridwell hit a single to center, and the Giant runner at third scored easily with the winning run.

Merkle, meanwhile, had started for second base, but when he saw the winning run cross the plate, he wheeled and ran for the Giants' clubhouse, just as he had after every other home game. That turned out to be a tragic mistake. Under the rules of baseball, to make the game-winning run official, he had to touch second base.

Not only Merkle, but everyone else thought the game was over and the Giants had won. But Johnny Evers of the Cubs knew the rules of baseball, and he saw that Merkle hadn't completed his run to second. Evers screamed at Artie Hofman, the Cubs' center fielder, to retrieve the ball. Hofman did and threw it in. But the Giants' third-base coach, Joe McGinnity, suspecting what Evers had in mind, ran out and intercepted the throw. He turned and threw the game ball high into the bleachers. The umpires weren't aware of these events because they had retired to their dressing room. Like the players, they didn't relish a confrontation with the rowdy fans who had invaded the field.

When McGinnity threw the ball into the stands, some observers claim that Evers found another ball and ran over to touch second base with it. Others say it never happened. The Cubs' manager, Frank Chance, rushed to the umpires' room and urged them to return to the field, where thousands of fans were celebrating the Giants' victory.

Chance convinced the umps that Merkle hadn't run to second and that Evers had retrieved the ball and touched the base for the third out. He tried to convince them that the game should be forfeited to Chicago because of the lack of crowd control. Hank

O'Day, the senior umpire, was easily persuaded, even though he'd witnessed very little. He agreed with Chance that Merkle was indeed out and that the run would be disallowed. He refused to forfeit the game to Chicago, declaring it a 1–1 tie.

For the next two days the uproar continued. League officials discussed the controversial game and finally upheld the head umpire. It was decided that if the two teams were locked in a tie for the championship at the end of the season, a playoff game would be necessary to break the tie.

As it turned out, a playoff was necessary. The Giants swooned in the final few days and lost five games. Three of those losses were to one man, pitcher Harry Coveleski of the Phillies, who beat them three times in one week and earned forever the nickname Giant Killer. In the playoff game the Cubs' Mordecai Brown, a 29-game winner, beat the Giants' Christy Mathewson, who had won 37.

Fred Snodgrass, a star player on that Giants team, once told baseball historian Lawrence Ritter that Giant Killer was a good name for Coveleski. But a cruel nickname to come out of that season was Bonehead in reference to Fred Merkle. "It was most unfair," Snodgrass was quoted, "to blame Freddie for our losing the pennant that season. Mostly it was the newspapermen who did it. Management never blamed him and neither did his teammates, not one of them. He was a fine boy and a very intelligent boy. But for the rest of his life everywhere he went he had to hear about that 'bonehead' play he made in 1908."

Blue Jays Blast
10 Homers in One Game

UNTIL SEPTEMBER 14, 1987, no major league team had slugged more than eight homers in a single game. The New York Yankees set the mark with eight dingers against the Philadelphia A's in 1939. Subsequently six other clubs equaled the record, the most recent being the Montreal Expos with an eight-homer day against the Atlanta Braves on July 30, 1978.

The Blue Jays shattered the mark during an 18–3 clobbering of the Baltimore Orioles in Toronto in 1987. In the second inning Jays catcher Ernie Whitt opened the barrage with a shot into the right-field bleachers, the first of three homers he collected in the game. Left fielder George Bell and third baseman Rance Mulliniks each added a pair of round-trippers to the attack, and solo homers went to center fielder Lloyd Moseby and two rookies, outfielder Rob Ducey and designated hitter Fred McGriff.

Ernie Whitt, perhaps the most popular Toronto Blue Jay of all time. Too bad he never got the chance to share in the Jays' World Series triumph. (Action Photographics)

Not only did the Blue Jays set a new standard of 10 homers in one game, but when Baltimore's Mike Hart homered in the third, the two clubs tied a mark for most home runs by two teams in a single game. In 1950 the Yankees (with six) and the Tigers (with five) collected 11 homers in nine innings of play.

Eleven Runs on One Hit

IF THERE WAS EVER A BASEBALL inning that never seemed to end, it took place in a game between the Kansas City Athletics and the Chicago White Sox on April 22, 1959. The teams approached the seventh inning with the A's trailing Chicago 8–6. The White Sox were known as a light-hitting team — a Chicago reporter once described a White Sox rally as a walk, a stolen base, a wild pitch, and a passed ball — but the Sox didn't need to rely on their bats to make history against Kansas City. In that memorable seventh inning three Kansas City pitchers took care of that.

The White Sox turned the seventh inning into a nightmare for the trio of A's hurlers. The Athletics sent Tom Gorman to the mound to start the inning. Ray Boone, the first White Sox batter, grounded to A's shortstop Joe DeMaestri, whose wild throw to first gave the Sox their first base runner. The next batter, Al Smith, tried to sacrifice Boone, but on the play the A's second baseman bobbled the ball, leaving runners on first and second with nobody out. Johnny Callison then singled to score Boone from second, but Kansas City outfielder Roger Maris misplayed the ball, another run scored, and Callison slid into third. Next, pitcher Gorman walked Luis Aparicio, who promptly stole second. To make matters worse, Gorman loaded the bases by issuing another free pass to opposing pitcher Bob Shaw.

That was all for Gorman. He got the hook and A's right-hander Mark Freeman came on in relief. Some relief! Freeman walked Earl Torgeson and Nellie Fox to force home two runs before his team recorded the first out. Freeman then walked Sherman Lollar, bringing home another run. Harry Craft, the frustrated manager of the A's, yanked Freeman and called on George Brunet to stem the tide. Incredibly Brunet was even wilder than his predecessors. He walked Boone, up for the second time in the inning, then walked four more batters and hit another with a pitch as the White Sox base runners paraded across home plate.

Finally the nightmare ended and the White Sox were retired. When the smoke cleared, the Sox had scored 11 runs on just one hit! Three Kansas City pitchers had given up 10 walks while the defence committed three errors. That was the season the White Sox captured their first American League pennant in 40 years.

A Wild Pitch Ruined His Season

IN 1904 PITCHER JACK CHESBRO was enjoying a brilliant season with the American League's New York Highlanders (later renamed the Yankees). He was almost unbeatable in winning a record 41 games. Despite Chesbro's heroics, the Highlanders needed to sweep a doubleheader from

Boston on the final day of the season. Two more wins would give them the league championship while a single Boston victory would turn the title over to the Red Sox.

Chesbro started the opener and pitched beautifully through eight innings. At that point the score was tied 2–2. In the ninth one of the Red Sox players reached first and advanced to third with two out. The Boston batter was shortstop Freddy Parent. Chesbro, a great spitball pitcher, loaded up the ball and heaved it toward his catcher's big mitt. But instead of dropping at the plate, as most spitters do, the ball took off and sailed over the catcher's head. The Boston runner scampered home from third with the winning run, the one that cinched the pennant.

Chesbro, whose nickname was Happy Jack because of his sunny disposition, was a Gloomy Gus on that afternoon. He was the goat of the game, after winning more games in a season than any hurler in this century.

Baseball's Highest Scoring Game

ON AUGUST 25, 1922, the Chicago Cubs and the Philadelphia Phillies met in what would become one of baseball's most memorable games. At the end of nine innings the Cubs had "squeezed out" a 26–23 triumph. The 49 runs scored in the game established an all-time record. The teams combined for 51 hits, and one player, Callaghan of the Cubs, came to bat three times in the same inning, a baseball first. Chicago had a 10-run inning and a 14-run inning.

The most runs any one team has scored in a game is 36. Back in 1897 Chicago beat Louisville 36–7. Recently, in a game between the Toronto Blue Jays and the Milwaukee Brewers at the SkyDome in August 1992, the Brewers amassed a record 31 hits in a 22–2 drubbing of the Jays. The total surpassed the previous American League mark, 30, set by the New York Yankees against the Boston Red Sox in 1923, and tied the major league record, achieved by the New York Giants in a game with the Cincinnati Reds in 1901.

Back-to-back No-hitters

DOZENS OF MAJOR LEAGUE PITCHERS have thrown no-hit, no-run games in the thousands that have been played, but only one has achieved two no-hitters in a row.

On June 15, 1938, nearly 40,000 fans filled Ebbets Field in Brooklyn for a game between the Dodgers and the Cincinnati Reds. Many were there to see the Dodgers face the pitches of Johnny Vander Meer, but most came to see the unique spectacle of an evening ball game, for this was the first game played in Brooklyn under the lights.

Just five days earlier the Cincinnati starter had tossed a no-hitter against Boston, and the name Vander Meer was on everyone's lips. But nobody expected he would work similar magic against the Dodgers. The record book showed that no pitcher had ever come up with two masterpieces in a row.

In fact, in the past, a no-hit mound gem was often followed by a mediocre or a losing performance.

But under the glare of the lights Vander Meer coasted through inning after inning. Suddenly it was the bottom of the ninth and he was three outs away from immortality.

At this critical stage of the game he tried to bear down a little bit harder. But the extra zip he put on his fastball cost him his control. He walked three of the Dodgers he faced in the ninth but somehow managed to get two outs. Then, with the crowd screaming, Brooklyn shortstop Leo Durocher dug in at the plate. Vander Meer took a deep breath, prayed his arm had one more strong pitch left in it, and delivered the ball. Durocher lashed at it, sending a fly ball into short center field. Reds outfielder Harry Craft raced in and made an easy catch for the final out.

Vander Meer was mobbed by his excited teammates. He had accomplished that rarest of pitching feats — two no-hitters in a row.

Durocher Didn't See Bobby Thomson's Blast

ONE OF THE MOST DRAMATIC home runs of all time was a three-run shot off the bat of Bobby Thomson on the afternoon of October 3, 1951. Thomson's rising line drive into the bleachers at the old Polo Grounds in New York terminated the most thrilling stretch run in baseball history, a duel for the National League pennant between the Giants and the Brooklyn Dodgers.

In August the Giants trailed the Dodgers by 13½ games when suddenly the New Yorkers caught fire, winning 37 of their final 44 games and finishing in a dead heat with their arch rivals. In a best-of-three playoff series the teams split the first two games. In the clincher, in the bottom of the ninth, the Giants trailed 4–1.

Giants manager Leo "Nice Guys Finish Last" Durocher trotted out to the third-base coaching lines for what he thought would be the last few minutes of the season. There was no reason to think that Dodger starter Don Newcombe would suddenly falter. Durocher had been needling the Dodger fireballer all afternoon. "Newcombe, you choke artist," he'd scream through cupped hands, trying to goad Newcombe into losing his composure. But Newcombe would just look over, as if to say, "Nice try, Leo. But I'm onto your tricks."

Then, three outs away from earning a World Series berth, Newcombe did show signs of weakening. Alvin Dark, the Giants' leadoff batter, singled. Don Meuller also singled. Then Monte Irwin, the Giants' best hitter, fouled out, but reliable Whitey Lockman came through with a smash into the left-field corner for a double, scoring Dark. Mueller twisted his ankle sliding into third, and Durocher, bouncing around the coaching box like an excited child, replaced him with pinch runner Clint Hartung. Meanwhile the fans were going crazy.

That was it for Newcombe. In from the bullpen strolled number 13, relief pitcher Ralph Branca. When Newcombe gave up the ball and left the mound, he took two big strides toward Durocher. Who could blame him if he wanted to throttle the mouthy little manager? But he settled for hurling a few choice curses at his tormentor and started for the clubhouse.

The next Giant batter was Bobby Thomson. While Branca was taking his warm-up pitches, Durocher ran up to Thomson. "Bobby," he said, "you drilled a homer off this guy in the first game of the playoffs. It was off his slider, so he won't be throwing it again. Look for his fastball, high and tight."

Thomson nodded, and sure enough, Branca's first pitch was right through Thomson's strike zone. Perfect. Except Thomson failed to swing. He looked down at Durocher, wide-eyed with anger, disgusted with himself for not swinging.

"Don't worry, kid!" Durocher shouted. "He's got another one just like that."

The second pitch flashed in, and Thomson's bat connected. The ball flew into left field, headed toward the lower deck of the Polo Grounds.

"You know, I didn't see it go in," Durocher would say later. "One of the greatest homers ever hit and I didn't see it. I thought it would hit the wall. Besides, I wasn't thinking home run. I was praying for a single to tie the score.

The New York Giants mob Bobby Thomson after his dramatic home run clinched the National League pennant in 1951.
(National Baseball Library)

"I sent Hartung home and waved Lockman in. Then I turned to spot the ball and there was no ball. The place was going nuts and fans were all over the field. One of them stole my hat and another threw a headlock on me that took all the breath out of me. I could have sworn I ran over to the stands and kissed my wife (Laraine Day, the actress), but she told me I never came near her.

"I remember how we all mobbed Bobby Thomson when he crossed home plate. What an incredible homer! People have been talking about it for decades. And I didn't even see it go in."

PART

3

CURIOUS
CHARACTERS

Marvelous Marv,
the Remarkable Met

HAS THERE EVER BEEN A WORSE CLUB than the New York Mets of 1962? Just look at their record. The stumblebums won only 40 games and lost 120, prompting manager Casey Stengel to cry, "Can't anybody here play this game?"

It wasn't just the number of games they lost. It was the way they lost them that drove Stengel batty and all Met fans to distraction. One of their most crushing defeats was a 15-inning marathon against the Phillies in which Met left-hander Al Jackson went all the way, allowing only three hits. The Mets lost in the bottom of the 15th on an error by — you guessed it — first baseman Marv Throneberry.

Every diehard Met fan has his own favorite disaster story of the 1962 season, and many of them revolved around Marvelous Marv Throneberry, a ball player said to have cast-iron hands and leaden feet. There was the time Marv booted a grounder in the first inning of a game to allow an unearned run. He came to bat in the bottom of the inning and tried to redeem himself by walloping a mammoth drive to the deepest part of the old Polo Grounds. As the ball rolled to the wall, Marv rounded first, raced by second, and then made a spectacular slide into third for a triple. The crowd screamed with joy.

But the opposing infielders claimed that Marv had failed to touch second base, and the umpire agreed. Throneberry was called out. New York manager Casey Stengel came trotting out of the dugout to argue the point, but before he got in his first word of complaint, the Mets' first-base coach intercepted him. "Don't bother, Casey," he sighed. "Marv didn't touch first base, either."

Baseball's Most Famous Mascot

EDDIE BENNETT WAS A REAL BASEBALL FAN, an engaging little guy with a hunchback. Years ago you would have found him seeking autographs outside the Polo Grounds in New York, home field for both New York clubs, the Giants and the Yankees.

One day in 1917 Happy Felsch, the Chicago White Sox star, playfully rubbed Eddie's misshapen back before a big game with the Yankees. "It'll bring us luck, Eddie," he said.

Apparently it did, for the White Sox won that day. Felsch rubbed Eddie's back again the next day, and again the White Sox won. Felsch brought Eddie right into the Chicago dugout for the third game, rubbed his back vigorously, and the Sox swept the series. Naturally lucky Eddie was given much of the credit, and he was promptly hired as the Chicago team mascot and batboy.

The White Sox went on to win the World Series that year, and Eddie Bennett became baseball's most talked-about good-luck charm. It wasn't long before the Brooklyn Dodgers lured him away from Chicago. Incredibly the Dodgers won the pennant in 1920 with Eddie on board. Then the Yankees enticed Eddie into their fold with a fancy salary. The Yanks promptly won three pennants in a row. After a two-year pause, they won three more.

By then Eddie Bennett was more famous and

more highly paid than many of the players. No batboy won more acclaim than the little hunchback who began his career by hanging around the player's entrance, seeking autographs and smiling self-consciously whenever a player gave him a friendly pat on the back.

The Doomed Diamond Star

ONE OF THE MOST DRAMATIC and certainly most tragic incidents connected with baseball took place back in 1902. It is the story of an unnamed Cherokee, an outstanding ball player, who, in the middle of the season, was found guilty by the chiefs of his nation of a serious crime. The punishment was harsh — death by hanging.

But the man's baseball skills were so remarkable that his team's manager was prompted to plead with the chiefs. Let the player rejoin the team, he asked, and play in as many games as possible until the date of execution.

The convicted man was called in front of the chiefs and asked for a solemn promise to return from his baseball duties at the appointed time. If he would make such a promise, his baseball career, short as it might be, would continue.

The Cherokee made the promise and rejoined his teammates. In the next few weeks he traveled through many states and played splendidly, even though each game brought him closer to his date with the hangman.

Finally there came a day when he packed his bag, waved farewell to his teammates, and made his way back to his tribe. As promised, he gave himself up to the men who'd sentenced him to die, and the following day the sentence was carried out.

The Curious Career of Charlie Faust

CHARLIE VICTOR FAUST BECAME a big league ball player because of a fortune-teller. Wearing his Sunday best, the Marion, Kansas, native walked out of the stands at old League Park in St. Louis on a July afternoon in 1911 and requested a tryout with the New York Giants, who were in town to play the St. Louis Cardinals. Faust had come to St. Louis on the advice of a fortune-teller, who had predicted he would become the greatest pitcher in baseball if he would help the Giants win the 1911 pennant.

Somehow Charlie Faust made an instant impression on manager John McGraw, even though his pitching skills were strictly minor league. In fact, his pitches were so slow that McGraw could catch them bare-handed. McGraw then had Faust take a turn at bat and ordered him to run the bases when he hit the ball so that his speed afoot could be measured. When Faust tapped the ball to the infield, the shortstop deliberately made a bad throw to first. Faust rounded the bag and went sliding into second. But the second baseman kicked the ball and Faust, up and running, slid into third. Another throwing error saw him set out for home, and again he slid in, kicking up dust.

When he arose, his best Sunday suit covered in dirt, the Giants enjoyed a big laugh at his expense. To their amazement McGraw decided to keep Faust around for the rest of the season and gave him a uniform. He predicted the newcomer would be a perfect good-luck charm. For the rest of the season Faust warmed up every day, thinking he might get a pitching assignment. But he never got to play.

When the Giants went on to win the pennant, McGraw credited the strange newcomer with bringing luck and harmony to his team. Faust was back the following season and continued to warm up every day. Once again the Giants won the pennant.

By then he was a huge attraction, and the fans urged McGraw to give him a chance. One day, against Cincinnati, McGraw did allow Faust to pitch. He hurled one inning late in the game and didn't seem the least bit surprised when the Reds couldn't hit his nothing-ball pitches. In the bottom half of the inning three Giants went down in order. But Faust was in the on-deck circle and everyone wanted to see him take his cuts. So the umpire broke the rules momentarily and allowed him to step in. For the first time in memory a team would need four outs to retire the side. Faust batted a slow roller to an infielder, and once again, through a number of messed-up plays, he toured the bases, sliding into each in a cloud of dust while the fans screamed his name.

When Faust left the Giants — he was gone four days to negotiate a contract to appear on Broadway — the team slumped and lost four straight games. In the Broadway show Faust, dressed in a Giants uniform, did imitations of major league stars like Ty Cobb and Honus Wagner. He was paid $400 a week to perform.

A few days later he was back with the team, baseball winning out over Broadway. Once more he warmed up every day without getting into a game, and once again the Giants won the pennant.

He became the most popular player who never played, and good fortune followed the Giants whenever he was around. But his own luck ran out in the winter of 1913 when the Giants discarded him. The following year Faust was declared insane and sent to an asylum, where he died in 1915. As for the Giants, they weren't the same without him. They lost the pennant in 1914 and failed to win it again until 1917.

Softball Star
Humbled at Hardball

IN 1955 FRED HUTCHISON, manager of the Seattle ball club of the Pacific Coast League, thought he'd found a partial answer to his team's pitching problems when he signed a hurler who'd struck out 11 major leaguers in a row. Hutchison almost drooled when he learned that the fastballer had recorded 55 no-hitters in the past 10 years.

The pitcher's name was Bob Fesler, and he was one of Seattle's top strikeout artists — at softball. In one appearance before a Pacific Coast League game Fesler's sizzling softballs struck out 11 of the baseball league's best batters, all in a row.

Even though Fesler was tossing them in from the softball distance — 45 feet — manager Hutchison was amazed at his prowess and signed him to a contract. What both manager and pitcher seemed to forget was that in baseball the pitcher has to throw from a mound. Fesler was accustomed to delivering his pitches from flat ground, as well as from a spot much closer to the plate. In his first start he allowed five hits, gave up five walks, made two wild pitches, and balked once. The opposing team scored five runs in the two-thirds of an inning he pitched. Hutchison gave Fesler a couple of more chances to adjust, but the results were equally disappointing, and the softball whiz went back to his first choice of diamond games with a record of 0–2.

Female Hurler Fans Ruth and Gehrig

NO WOMAN HAS EVER PLAYED major league baseball, but a slim teenager named Jackie Mitchell came close. On April 2, 1931, the Double A Chattanooga Lookouts played the New York Yankees in an exhibition game prior to the opening of the new season.

A few days before the contest the Lookouts had signed 17-year-old Jackie Mitchell, who had established herself as a star pitcher in high school and in semipro baseball. She didn't throw hard, but her pitches took a mean drop just before reaching the plate and her strikeout totals were impressive.

When the Lookouts' starting hurler got into trouble early in the game, the manager called on Mitchell. The first batter she faced was Babe Ruth. The crowd of 4,000 roared in anticipation of the unique confrontation. The first woman to play in a professional game was about to face the game's greatest star, with another legend, Lou Gehrig, standing in the on-deck circle.

Mitchell's first pitch to the Babe was a ball. The next two pitches looked good to Ruth. He swung at both and missed. Embarrassed, Ruth had the umpire examine the the ball. He couldn't believe a teenage girl could put two strikes past him without resorting to chicanery. But the umpire kept the ball in play. "It's clean, Babe," he told Ruth. "No cuts, no scuff marks, and no saliva."

Mitchell delivered the one-two pitch, and Ruth watched it drop at his knees. "STEEE-RIKE THREE!" the umpire bellowed. Ruth glared at the man in blue and threw down his bat while the crowd howled in glee. "The Babe was really upset," Mitchell later told reporters. "Mad as all get-out."

Next it was Gehrig's turn. Mitchell threw three sinkers, and Gehrig, swinging hard, missed all of them. He, too, took a slow walk back to the dugout. Tony Lazzeri, the next Yankee batter, fared better than his mates. He drew a walk on four pitches. The Chattanooga manager figured Mitchell should quit while she was ahead, so he removed her from the game while the crowd hailed her performance with a standing ovation.

In a postgame interview reporters asked Mitchell if she thought the Yankee sluggers were really trying or were they deliberately missing her sinker balls. "Damn right they were trying," Mitchell snorted. "Better hitters than them couldn't hit me. Why should it be any different because they're Yankees?"

Unfortunately Mitchell's feat didn't earn her a professional contract. She continued to play semi-pro ball in Chattanooga for another six years when she retired to enter the business world. Long after her playing career was over Mitchell was often called upon to talk about how she became the first woman to play in a professional baseball game and how she fanned two of the game's most brilliant players.

The Lady in the Batter's Box

THEY SAID IT COULD NEVER HAPPEN — a woman stepping up to the plate in a major league game! But it did happen once.

Her name was Kitty Burke, and she made baseball history on July 31, 1935, during a game in Cincinnati. Burke, a blond nightclub singer, was among the thousands of fans who elbowed their way into the Cincinnati ballpark to see the Reds face the Cardinals "under the lights." Night baseball was new to the major leagues, and the novelty attracted overflow crowds.

On this night special trains brought thousands of fans to Cincinnati from outlying areas. The trains fell behind schedule, and when they finally arrived, the fans aboard leaped off and rushed to the ballpark, only to find that all of the seats had been sold. Larry MacPhail, the Reds' general manager, greeted the estimated 10,000 out-of-towners and ushered them into the stadium. What else could he possibly do? Many of them held tickets to the game, and MacPhail could hardly admit he'd allowed other fans to fill their seats.

MacPhail herded the late arrivals onto the field. He lined a few thousand along the foul lines while hundreds more crowded in behind the plate, so close to the batter's box they were almost breathing down the umpire's neck.

Players on both clubs risked injury and loss of uniform snagging routine catches along the foul lines and in making their way to the plate. Fans reached out and tried to grab their caps and gloves. A player executing a catch in among the spectators had to outwrestle a dozen fans just to keep possession of the ball.

Miss Kitty Burke, standing on her high heels near home plate, saw a chance to gain a prized souvenir of the game when the Reds' Babe Herman muscled his way through the crowd to get to the plate in the eighth inning. Burke grabbed the bat from Herman's hands and instructed her friends, "Hang on to him, boys. I'm going to take his turn at bat."

And so she did. Kitty strode to the plate, waved Herman's big bat at St. Louis pitcher Paul Dean, and shouted, "Throw it to me, big boy." Dean shrugged and lobbed the ball toward the plate. Kitty took a mighty swing and tapped the ball down the first-base line. Dean moved over, fielded it, and tagged out the high-heeled runner. The crowd booed Dean and cheered Burke as she was escorted off the diamond.

The incident took only a few seconds. The Reds weren't charged with an out, the game continued, and Kitty Burke's one-pitch at-bat was quickly forgotten. But her impetuous behavior that night made the name Kitty Burke the answer to one of baseball's most puzzling trivia questions: who is the only woman to come to bat in a major league game?

Heavyweight Champ
at First Base

OCCASIONALLY A STAR in one sport attempts to make his mark in another. In the 1890s one of boxing's biggest celebrities was Gentleman Jim Corbett, the heavyweight champ. Corbett won the title in 1892 by knocking out John L. Sullivan in 21 rounds.

But Corbett had always aspired to be a baseball player, and his love for the diamond game was well publicized. After he captured the heavyweight title, there were dozens of offers from team owners who assured him he could combine the two sports. Corbett said he was willing to try but only if he could display his skills while playing for many teams in several different leagues.

Between title fights the popular champion played in six different leagues and in dozens of exhibition games at all levels of baseball and was often promised half the gate receipts just for showing up. One of his stops was in Toronto where he went hitless in four trips, much to the disappointment of a huge crowd that turned out to see him play.

In the summer of 1897, playing first base for a number of minor league clubs, Corbett is said to have earned $17,000, a fortune in that era. Such was his fame that one of the batboys for a team he joined made extra money of his own by swatting mosquitoes on Corbett's back and selling them to fans for five cents apiece.

Corbett ended his diamond career after 26 official games in organized baseball. His career batting average was .262 and his fielding average was .943.

Whenever a brawl would break out on the field or in the stands, Corbett's fans would urge him to get involved, to wade in and throw a few of his famous knockout punches. But the heavyweight champion would simply smile and tip his cap to his supporters. He was content to let the "amateur" brawlers settle their differences in their own traditional way.

Baseball's Midget Hitters

WHEN THREE-FOOT, SEVEN-INCH Eddie Gaedel, wearing number ⅛ on his uniform, stepped up to the plate for the St. Louis Browns in the second game of a doubleheader with the Detroit Tigers in August 1951, he became the first midget ever to appear in a major league game.

Gaedel pinch-hit for Frank Saucier, whose entire career consisted of one hit in 14 at bats. Gaedel, as expected, drew four balls from Tiger pitcher Bob Cain who, understandably, had a hard time finding the strike zone. After being replaced on first by pinch runner Jim Delsing, Gaedel trotted off the field never to return.

Later, when asked if he had considered swinging at one of Cain's pitches, Gaedel said, "No, because Mr. Veeck told me he'd be up on the stadium roof with a high-powered rifle, and if I so much as looked like I was going to swing, he said he'd shoot me dead."

A strange parallel to the Gaedel incident occurred in a 1905 minor league game between Buffalo and Baltimore. Buffalo manager George Stallings befriended a midget named Jerry Sullivan, who was staying in their Baltimore hotel. Sullivan was playing the part of Little Mose in a popular musical of the day, and Stallings invited him out to the park to act as the team's mascot.

Sullivan wore a special Buffalo uniform tailored for him by the acting company, and he prowled the coaching lines for two innings. With Buffalo trailing 10–2 in the ninth and with a runner on base, Stallings called back pitcher Stan Yerkes. To everyone's amazement the manager sent Sullivan to the plate. Using a regulation bat, the diminutive pinch hitter guided the second pitch over the third baseman's head. A single, a wild pitch, and another single brought Sullivan home with a headfirst slide. He rose from the dust to a standing ovation, then returned to the theater, his baseball career at an end but still the proud owner of a perfect lifetime batting average.

As for Eddie Gaedel, he lived the remaining 10 years of his life off his brief celebrity and died tragically in Chicago following a savage mugging. Pitcher Bob Cain was baseball's only representative at the funeral. "I never even met him, but I felt obligated to go," Cain said.

Eddie Gaedel, at three foot, seven inches and 65 pounds, made his one big league appearance at bat for the St. Louis Browns in 1951.

(National Baseball Library)

Youngest Batter
Robbed by Umpire

WILLIE DIGGINS WAS NINE YEARS OLD in 1905 when a bizarre series of incidents led to his becoming the youngest player in history to perform for a professional team.

Willie's father, Bill, was the catcher for the Manchester team in the New England League, and Willie was often allowed to sit on the bench during his dad's games. In a game against arch rival Lowell, Willie's father allowed a passed ball with the bases loaded, then proceeded to stumble and fall while chasing it. The go-ahead run scored on the play, and the Manchester manager was so angry at Diggins's clumsiness that he banished the embarrassed catcher to the showers.

But he'd forgotten that three of his other players had been tossed by the umpire earlier in the game. As a result, he had no spare players on the bench. Spotting nine-year-old Diggins sitting there, he offered him five dollars to go and stand in right field. The kid didn't say a word. He just grabbed a glove and hustled out.

No Lowell batters were able to send any balls in Diggins's direction, but the youngster's hitting talents were tested in the final inning. Trailing by a run, Manchester loaded the bases. With two out it was Willie's turn at the plate. The manager wisely told him to keep the bat on his shoulder. "Kid, you're so small the pitcher will walk you," he was told. "So don't even think of swinging."

Sure enough, the pitcher had trouble finding Willie's strike zone, and his first two offerings were balls. Then he lobbed a ball that floated to the plate.

Young Willie couldn't resist and lunged at the pitch, missing by a foot. Two balls, one strike.

The manager cupped his hands and screamed at Willie, "Kid, I told you to keep the bat on your shoulder!"

Willie watched three more pitches go by, two of them balls, the third a called strike. The count was three and two. One more ball and Willie would walk, bringing in the tying run.

The next pitch sailed over Willie's head. "Strike three!" the ump called. Willie was out and the game was over.

At that point young Willie had to scamper out of the way because the Manchester manager, howling like a rabid wolf, made a dash for the umpire. He was brandishing a baseball bat, and before the man in blue could turn and flee, he struck the arbiter in the chest and knocked him flat. Players from both teams quickly intervened while an astonished Willie Diggins looked on. It was a violent ending to his only appearance in a professional baseball game.

Handicapped Players Have Made Their Mark

JIM ABBOTT IS SUCH A GOOD PITCHER that few fans are even aware he plays one-handed. Born with only a partial right arm, he persevered to become one of baseball's premier southpaws. Abbott fields ground balls by quickly switching his glove from under his right arm to his left and back again.

The American League's designated hitter rule relieves him of the need to bat one-handed, but such was not the case for St. Louis Browns out-fielder Pete Gray, who played 77 games in 1945 despite having only one arm. Gray had lost his left arm in a childhood accident but realized his dream to be a major league ball player during the war when call-ups decimated lineups. He managed a .218 bat-ting average and spent many seasons, both before and after 1945, playing in a variety of minor league towns.

Playing with the use of only one arm is difficult enough, but for Bert Shepard the challenge was learning to pitch on an artificial leg. In the thirties pitcher Monty Stratton had attempted a comeback after losing a leg in a hunting accident. He never again appeared in a major league game, but his story inspired a movie starring James Stewart. It also inspired Shepard.

In 1941 Shepard, a gifted left-hander, enlisted in the air force right after the Japanese bombed Pearl Harbor on December 7. He was shot down on a bombing mission over Europe and German doctors were forced to amputate his right leg.

When the Allies liberated his POW camp, Shep-ard returned to America determined to make a baseball comeback. Although somewhat restricted in movement by his artificial limb, he was given a tryout by the Washington Senators and proved to be as mobile as any other pitcher in fielding bunts or covering first base. Shepard's first exhibition game victory over Brooklyn was tainted somewhat by Dodger manager Leo Durocher's orders that his team not bunt.

When the regular season got under way, the Sen-ators were reluctant to take a chance on the war hero. It appeared he would suffer the same fate as

Stratton. Finally Washington manager Ossie Bluege relented and on August 4 Shepard took the mound for his only major league appearance. Pitching five innings, he struck out two and allowed only one run for a career ERA of 1.69.

Shepard returned to the minors, and a series of operations at Walter Reed Army Hospital restricted his career until 1949 when he signed as playing manager of a Class B team. His popularity was such that players raised money from local merchants to prevent his release when management could no longer afford his $4,500 salary. Shepard posted a 5–6 record and filled in at first base. Not only did he hit .229 but incredibly he stole five bases.

New York Giants Travel 800 Miles to Convocation

PRINCE HAL SCHUMACHER WAS A CAREER pitcher (159–120) for the New York Giants from 1931 to 1946 and went 2–2 in three World Series, but it is doubtful that any of these records matched the thrill of his third major league season in 1933. On an off day in June in the midst of a pennant race the Giants took an 800-mile round trip to Canton, New York, for St. Lawrence University's convocation ceremonies.

Schumacher had earned his degree at St. Lawrence while a member of the Giants, and manager Bill Terry, recognizing the significance of such an achievement, supported the decision to send the team to Canton for the day. Schumacher had pitched at the college and also for a local semipro team, the Spofford Hose Company of the Dolgeville

Volunteer Fire Department, where he'd been scouted by the Giants.

The Giants' decision to attend Schumacher's graduation ceremony electrified the university and the village. Plans were confirmed for an exhibition game between the collegians and the Giants and seating was expanded for 8,000. Pathé News cameras arrived to record the event, which was shown a few days later in movie houses throughout the country. Graham MacNamee, the outstanding sports announcer of the day, described the convocation on a live radio broadcast.

Schumacher took his place in Gunnison Memorial Chapel with the 108 other members of the class. Loudspeakers broadcast the ceremony to those sitting on the lawn outside. Inside, spectators included the entire New York Giants ball club and Schumacher's parents, who had emigrated from Germany 30 years before.

Afterward those in attendance jostled for the honor of having their photo taken with the famous Giants and their lineup of stars, including future Hall of Famers Mel Ott, Travis Jackson, and Terry, the last man to hit .400 or better in the National League. If other graduates and their parents felt somewhat miffed at the attention garnered by Schumacher and his famous friends, they didn't say. Most of them lined up to take pictures of the New York guests.

The game was somewhat of an anticlimax after the pomp and circumstance that attended the awarding of the Bachelor of Science degree to Schumacher, but he did pitch two innings as the Giants rolled over their amateur competition 12–4.

Less than a month later Prince Hal was named to

the National League team for the very first All-Star game. That fall he would pitch the second game of the World Series. He finished the season with 19 victories, including seven shutouts, and an ERA of 2.16. For all his 1933 accomplishments he was paid the princely sum of $3,000.

And of the event which is still spoken of by old-timers in upstate New York, noted sportswriter Bob Considine called it "one of the rare pieces of sentiment our national pastime has produced."

Waddell Puts Punch into Acting

OLD-TIME PITCHER RUBE WADDELL once starred in a stage play called *The Stain of Guilt,* and his fame was such that he drew packed houses to his performances. In no time at all Waddell learned to dress like the famous actors of the early 1900s, buying himself a fur coat, a top hat, and a fancy cane.

Waddell's debut in his off-season career was memorable. An important scene took place in a hotel room. The villain had tracked down the heroine and was choking the life out of her. Suddenly the hero (Waddell) burst through the door, shouting, "Unhand that maiden, you cur!" Then he leaped upon the villain, and was supposed to knock his opponent down with a stage blow and rescue the girl.

But Waddell never did things by halves. On opening night he worked himself into an appropriate rage for the big scene. When he struck the villain, he swung from the floor and knocked the poor chap across the stage and into the orchestra pit. The man landed on the bass drum and demolished it. He was semiconscious and his jaw was so swollen that he could barely speak. Alas, there was no understudy and the performance had to be canceled. The following day the producer of the play hired an understudy for the villain, the orchestra leader purchased a new drum, and the director took Waddell aside for a quick course in stage punching.

Waddell was one of the game's wackiest eccentrics, a fact Lee Allen aptly chronicles in *The American League Story,* where he writes that Rube began the year of his acting "celebrity" sleeping in "a firehouse at Camden, New Jersey, and ended it tending bar in a saloon in Wheeling, West Virginia. In between these events he won 22 games for the Philadelphia Athletics, played left end for the Business Men's Rugby Football Club of Grand Rapids, Michigan, toured the nation in a melodrama called *The Stain of Guilt,* courted, married, and became separated from May Wynne Skinner of Lynn, Massachusetts, saved a woman from drowning, accidentally shot a friend through the hand, and was bitten by a lion."

Anson the Actor

BACK IN THE LATE 19TH CENTURY the Chicago White Stockings' Adrian "Cap" Anson was the first major league ball player to play the lead in a stage play. In fact, the play, called *A Runaway Colt,* was written with Anson in mind. The script called for the Hall of Fame first baseman and manager to be enamored of a banker's daughter, a young woman who returned his affections despite the objections of her father.

In one scene the father confronts Anson and says, "My little Bertha may love you, but I have little use for ball players. I've decided to give you a chance to prove your worth as a suitor. If you win the big game tomorrow, I'll allow you to continue courting my Bertha. If you lose, you must agree to never darken our door again."

Anson agreed, and in the next scene he was at bat onstage. The game was in the final inning, and if Anson homered, his team would win. A stagehand pitched the ball from the wings, and Anson hit it out of sight, somewhere in behind the curtains.

He began his home run gallop around the bases, all three of which were invisible to the audience. Then he disappeared into the wings where voices could be heard cheering him on. Eventually he appeared at the other end of the stage and ended his run with a fancy slide into home plate just as the catcher caught the ball. An umpire called him safe. Anson had won the game — and the girl. No production had a happier ending.

The play earned solid reviews, and when it opened in New York, Anson decided to augment the cast. He persuaded some of baseball's biggest stars to join him onstage — Willie Keeler, Arlie Latham, and Joe Kelley. They would help make the play a big success on Broadway.

The famous baseball scene began, and Anson, with a perfect swing, hit the ball out of sight and started for first base. He disappeared behind the curtains and a few moments later burst from the wings and began his slide into home plate. Just then the ball landed in the mitt of Keeler, who was covering home, and he tagged Anson hard. Latham, who had taken over the role of the umpire, yelled dramatically, "You're out!"

The audience roared with laughter as Anson snarled at Latham, "What do you mean, out? I can't be out."

"You were out by a foot," Latham insisted.

Meanwhile the stage manager rushed onstage and grabbed Latham by the mask. "You fool!" he shouted. "That's not in the script." The director joined him and berated Keeler and Kelley. Both ball players stood there grinning at the irate theater men. A furious Anson leaped to his feet and threatened to tear apart all three veterans.

Finally some semblance of order was restored and the stage manager approached the footlights. "Ladies and gentlemen," he announced, "the umpire has just informed me that the ball used to tag Mr. Anson out at the plate was not the one he hit. The ball Mr. Anson hit was so well struck that it has not been found yet. So the umpire has reversed his decision and declared Mr. Anson safe at home. Mr. Anson wins the game and the lovely Bertha. And that marks the end of this performance. Thank you."

Cap Anson continued starring in the play for several weeks. But never again did he invite other baseball players to share the spotlight with him.

Moe Berg, Scholar, Spy, Catcher

MOE BERG, THE OUTSTANDING JEWISH catcher, had a fascinating life on and off the field. He is the only ball player who agreed to become a cold-blooded assassin in one of his escapades away from the diamond.

Berg was born in 1902 and grew up to be an athlete, scholar, and government spy. By the time he graduated from Princeton, he was fluent in a dozen languages. He was offered a teaching position with the university but declined, opting instead for a career in professional baseball.

After some time in the minors, he was acquired by the Chicago White Sox. By then Berg had finished a year at Columbia Law School and eventually he became partner in a Wall Street law firm.

In 1932 he visited Japan and added Japanese to a growing list of languages he spoke. When he returned to Japan in 1934 as a player on an all-star team that included Babe Ruth and Lou Gehrig, he was able to pass along coaching tips to Japanese college players in their own language. In Tokyo he slipped away to a local hospital on the pretext of visiting the U.S. ambassador's daughter, went to the roof of the hospital, and filmed the city's skyline with a small movie camera. During World War II, the film was used in planning air raids against Tokyo.

Berg's father, angry because his son had chosen a career in baseball, never attended a game. On January 14, 1942, the day his father died, Berg quit baseball and went to work for the U.S. government.

He was recruited by the Office of Strategic Services, forerunner of the CIA, as an intelligence agent. It was thought his fame as a ball player would be an ideal cover for his work as a spy.

In Italy he once impersonated a German officer and was allowed to inspect an Italian munitions factory. On leaving the site he grumbled that Berlin was unhappy with the plant's production levels.

In 1944 Berg invited top scientist Werner Heisenberg to speak at a conference in Switzerland. Berg's assignment: to find out how close Germany was to manufacturing an atom bomb. If the scientist sounded confident that such a bomb would soon be unleashed, Berg was prepared to pull out a concealed pistol and assassinate the man. But when Heisenberg mentioned no such plans and rambled on about Germany losing the war, Berg decided to spare his life.

Berg might have written a book about his cloak-and-dagger adventures, plus his career in baseball, had not a deal with the publisher turned sour. The catcher walked away from it when he discovered the senior editor who offered him a $35,000 contract had confused him with Moe of the Three Stooges.

PART

4

TRICKS AND TRIVIA OF THE TRADE

North African Berbers Invented Baseball?

EVEN ABNER DOUBLEDAY NEVER CLAIMED to have invented baseball. After all, forms of the game had been played a century before in England. But where did those early games come from? Popular theory suggested they had their roots in English village games of the Middle Ages, but in 1937 an Italian anthropologist, Corrado Gini, provided an even more antique reference.

On an expedition in the Libyan desert to investigate a mysterious strain of blondness among Berber tribes, he found tribesmen in the village of Jadum playing what even he, with his limited knowledge of sports and games, recognized as a rudimentary form of baseball. The tribesmen's game required a level playing field with a home base separated from a running base by 70 to 90 feet. The batting team, hitting in order, struck a ball as far as possible so that the other members of the team could run back and forth between home and the running base. Caught flies and missed strikes were part of the game.

So how did this North African game eventually make it to America? Gini concluded that the Berber game was actually a kind of living fossil left by Norse invaders some 8,000 years previously. The African game was similar to old Norse games like longball and northern spell, which were used as fertility rites to celebrate spring's return and ensure a plentiful harvest. Eventually forms of these games made their way to England where they evolved into the village sport of rounders.

When cricket became England's most popular

Early ball game. Note the lack of baseball gloves.
(Virginia State Library)

adult bat-and-ball game in the 18th century, rounders stagnated and remained a children's activity until it crossed the ocean to America. Here it found new life at New England town hall meetings and was called townball.

It was a variation of this game that was played in small towns such as Cooperstown, New York, until the 1840s when Alexander Cartwright and his friends with the Knickerbocker Volunteer Fire Company established a club, wrote out some rules, and gradually came to legitimize baseball as an adult recreation.

The Doubleday myth awaited the patronage of sporting goods entrepreneur and former big league pitcher Albert Spalding, who formed a blue ribbon committee to fix a time, place, and originator of the game. Relying mainly on the muddled story of a Denver, Colorado, resident, historian Abner Graves, the committee published its report in 1907, concluding that Doubleday had invented the game in 1839 in Cooperstown, New York.

Although every authority since has refuted the commission's concoction, Cooperstown's place in American folklore, and as home of baseball's Hall of

Fame, ensures that the legend will probably live forever.

Baseball's First Pro Team

AMERICA'S FIRST PROFESSIONAL BALL CLUB was the Cincinnati Red Stockings, a team organized in 1869 by an English-born cricket star named Harry Wright. The versatile Wright learned all about baseball growing up in New York. He not only managed the Red Stockings but performed in sensational style as his team's center fielder, relief pitcher, and captain.

In 1869, having signed many of the best players in the nation to professional contracts, Wright led this club on a cross-country tour, taking on all challengers. By the time the Redlegs reached California, they had accumulated a record 44 victories and no defeats. Their uniforms — white flannel shirts with a red C on the chest, white linen caps, white knickers, and red stockings — were revolutionary and drew admiring glances from all who saw them play.

In San Francisco, where they played three games in four days, plus a five-hour cricket match, they met the strongest opposition the state could offer, the best of more than 50 teams in the Bay area. The awesome team from the East defeated the Eagles 35–4 and 58–4 and were leading the Pacifics 66–4 when dusk arrived. Wright had his men deliberately hit into outs to bring the game to a merciful conclusion. The visitors from Ohio won other games by scores of 54–5, 76–5, and 46–14.

The tour of the Red Stockings was so successful

that their exploits were flashed by telegraph to cities across North America, and they became known as the Invincible Nine. But they were invincible for only the one season. By 1870 other professional teams sprang up — teams named Brown Stockings, Blue Stockings, and Green Stockings. Several of the new pro clubs, including the Chicago White Stockings, were able to beat the Cincinnati boys. By 1871 an association of pro clubs was formed, and within five years the National League, baseball's first professional body, was in operation.

Canadian Introduces Baseball Glove

ART IRWIN, ALSO KNOWN AS FOXY ART, Doc, Artful Arthur, and Cut-rate Irwin, left a memorable store of baseball achievements. But he is best-known for popularizing the baseball glove.

The Toronto-born Irwin was an acclaimed shortstop. The *New York Clipper* once noted that "his fielding in the Worcester–Cincinnati contest of August 31, 1880, was phenomenal, he accepting all fifteen chances offered him, and assisting no fewer than thirteen times." The account suggests nothing extraordinary except that in those days players performed without gloves, a condition Irwin rectified a few seasons later as a member of the Providence Grays.

A hard-hit ball broke two of his left-hand fingers, and Irwin, risking the inevitable calls of "sissy" and "Mama's boy," bought a buckskin glove several sizes too big. He added some padding and fitted his two broken digits into one of the glove's roomy spaces.

Irwin played when others may have sat, and he helped his team win a pennant. Within two years most ball players had adopted the "Irwin Glove."

The Canadian was a true innovator who helped to lead the player revolt of 1890, introduced professional baseball to Cuba, managed, scouted, and even umpired on occasion. He even wrote a player's guide to the game.

Irwin was one of the truly fascinating characters of early baseball, but his life ended tragically. Apparently depressed about his inability to maintain two marriages at the same time, he jumped overboard and drowned while sailing between New York and Boston. The various baseball encyclopedias refer to his burial place as, simply, the Atlantic Ocean.

More About Gloves

BASEBALL WRITER DAVID KINDRED, writing in *The Sporting News,* says he owns the best baseball glove ever made, the Wilson A2000. It was the last glove he bought and cost him $35, which was a week's pay back in 1962. He still recalls the painful moment when he ran hard, glove up, to make a game-ending catch, only to feel the baseball thud against the heel of his glove and fall into fair territory. It had been a high pop-up into the sun, with two men out, a three-and-two count on the batter, bases loaded, and everybody moving on the pitch. Kindred will never forget that agonizing instant. All of the base runners scored.

Since then he has done some research into gloves and discovered that:

- Babe Ruth's first glove in reform school was a catcher's mitt, which he wore backward on his right hand.
- Joe Morgan played forever with a glove barely larger than his hand because Nellie Fox told him a second baseman couldn't afford to lose the ball in a normal-sized glove.
- Rogers Hornsby folded his glove and stuck it in his rear pocket while batting.
- Ozzie Smith's first glove was a brown paper bag.
- Catcher Dick Buckley padded his big mitt with a sheet of lead.
- Dick "Dr. Strangeglove" Stuart's first baseman's glove failed him so often that the mayor of Pittsburgh wanted first base declared a disaster area.
- Brooklyn's Babe Herman, with a reputation like Stuart's as a poor glove man, and sensitive to accusations of outfield incompetence, once declared he would quit the game if a fly ball ever hit him on the head. A teammate asked, "How about the shoulder, Babe?" And Herman replied, "On the shoulder don't count."

Snorts Kindred, "Now they're making gloves like sneakers. You can pump them up with air to improve the fit. The Japanese have even experimented with a catcher's mitt that emits an electronic beam that turns on a light in the pitcher's glove as a signal for the next pitch."

Death on the Diamond

DURING A GAME ON AUGUST 16, 1920, Ray Chapman, the 29-year-old shortstop for the Cleveland Indians, was hit on the head by a pitch thrown by Carl Mays of the New York Yankees. Chapman died the following day. In the thousands of games that have been played in the major leagues, and counting the hundreds of batters who have been brushed back, beaned, and bent out of shape by pitched balls, it is amazing that only one player — Ray Chapman — has been fatally injured.

Chapman was the most popular man on his team and was the leading hitter among American League shortstops, with a .303 average that year. In the opinion of experts he was headed for a berth in the Hall of Fame. Two dozen priests and hundreds of fans attended his funeral.

Chapman had been contemplating retirement at the end of the season. His wife was pregnant and his millionaire father-in-law had proposed that he enter the family business. His untimely death prevented him from completing the greatest season of his career, for Cleveland went on to win the American League pennant and the 1920 World Series.

Carl Mays had a reputation for brushing batters back with his submarine deliveries, but he denied throwing deliberately at Chapman. Unlike the deceased, he wasn't a popular player and he was often accused of not showing sufficient remorse over the fact that one of his errant pitches led to baseball's only fatality.

Soon after Chapman's death umpires were instructed to replace balls that became scuffed or discolored. It was felt that Chapman had been hit by a dirty baseball, one he couldn't see well as it flew toward him and ended his life.

The Seventh-inning Stretch

I T IS AS MUCH A PART OF BASEBALL tradition as the national anthem, the scoreboard, and the hot dog. It is the seventh-inning stretch, that time in the game when fans feel an urge to rise from their seats en masse and, well, stretch.

The inventor of the seventh-inning stretch was American president William Howard Taft, who was elected in 1908 and attended as many ball games as possible. But he was seldom comfortable at games, primarily because he was an extremely fat individual and found the seats to be too hard and confining. So, after a few innings, he would hoist his 300-pound body erect and stretch his arms and legs. In most cases it happened to be the seventh inning when Taft lumbered to his feet. Those around him followed suit, of course, and before long the seventh-inning stretch became a familiar practice at every ball game.

If Taft were president today and wanted to stretch, he would probably introduce the fifth-inning stretch, since modern-day ball games are about 45 minutes longer than they were 80 years ago.

But stretching at ball games isn't the only innovation Taft introduced to the game. In 1910 he became the first president to throw out the initial pitch on opening day.

The Spitter
and the Eephus Pitch

FORKBALLS, KNUCKLEBALLS, SLIDERS, split-fingered fastballs, and spitballs — baseball pitchers are always seeking new ways to deliver the ball to make batters look foolish.

All of the above are legal except the spitter, a pitch invented in 1902 by George Hildebrand, an outfielder. Hildebrand taught the pitch to a Sacramento teammate, Elmer Stricklett, whose career was skidding downhill because of arm problems. With the spitter Stricklett returned to the majors and became a winner again.

The pitch was despised by batters, and along with all substance pitches, including the shine ball, it was banned in 1920. Not only did such pitches have a tendency to break in unpredictable ways on their flight from the mound to the plate, but the ball, which was seldom replaced in those days, got dirty quickly, thus making it difficult for batters to see. This is one of the reasons cited for Ray Chapman's death following a beaning in 1920.

For reasons known only to scientists spit on a ball causes wind resistance to vary on different sides of the ball, leading to its unpredictable movement. Many early-day players built their careers on this unusual pitch.

Seventeen spitball pitchers active in 1920 were allowed to continue using the pitch to the end of their careers. By the 1930s only Red Faber, Clarence Mitchell, Jack Quinn, and Burleigh Grimes remained legal spitballers. Mitchell was the first to retire in 1932, followed the next year by Quinn and Faber.

Grimes, who produced abundant saliva with the aid of a huge wad of gum, was a true master who accumulated 270 wins and four 20-win seasons before retiring at the end of 1934.

Even though it is supposed to be as dead as the dinosaur, the illegal spitball continues to be thrown by pitchers who know just how difficult it is to catch them in the act. Dodger ace Preacher Roe admitted as much in a magazine article after he retired in 1954.

Perhaps the most famous gimmick pitch was the "eephus ball," an invention of Pittsburgh Pirate hurler Rip Sewell in 1941. Sewell was able to deliver a ball that soared as high as 25 feet before it dropped sharply and crossed the plate, leaving the poor batter transfixed. One of Sewell's teammates named the pitch. "It's an eephus because it's a nothin' pitch and an eephus ain't nothin'" was his explanation.

The first time Sewell threw his eephus ball in a big league game was in the ninth inning of a contest between the Pirates and the Cubs. The Pirates were ahead 2–1, the bases were loaded, and Dom Dallessandro of the Cubs was at the plate. The count on him was three and two.

It was no time to experiment with a freak pitch, but Sewell thought he'd go for broke and unveil the eephus ball. The horsehide left his hand and soared like a balloon. It wobbled high in the air, 25 feet up. The batter lowered his hands and gawked. So did the umpire, the other players, and the fans. Suddenly the ball began to plummet, and before Dallessandro could set himself, the eephus dropped across the center of the plate.

"Strike three!" the umpire roared.

"Son of a bitch!" Dallessandro said, walking away in disgust. He took a few steps, then raised his bat and pointed it at Sewell. "If this bat was a rifle, I'd shoot your bleepin' head off," he snarled.

Russell Ford Finds a Career-saving Pitch

SHORTLY AFTER THE TURN of the century, while Henry Ford was winning fame and fortune for his revolutionary ideas as an automaker, a ball player named Russell Ford (no relation) was doing his bit to revolutionize the art of pitching baseballs.

It was 1908 and pitcher Ford, a minor leaguer, was just another hurler, an unlikely candidate for major league stardom. Ford, a member of the Atlanta Crackers in the Southern Association, was tossing some leisurely warm-up pitches one day when the ball skipped away from his catcher and bounced off a concrete post. The ball was badly scuffed, and when Ford got it back and tried a few more pitches with it, he got the surprise of his life. His fastball hopped in midflight and his curveball dipped at the plate as it never had before.

Ford realized his entire future in baseball hinged on this accidental discovery. He began experimenting with a number of baseballs, using broken glass from beer bottles to roughen one side of the balls. When he pitched, batters swung and missed, while Ford's scuffed balls, hopping and dropping, made them blink and groan in frustration.

Within two seasons Ford had moved to the majors and became a valuable starting pitcher with the New York Yankees. By then he was secretly using emery cloth, sewn into the webbing of his glove, as the abrasive material required to scuff the ball and make its flight to the plate an erratic and unpredictable journey.

In his debut as a Yankee he hurled a 1–0 shutout over the Philadelphia Athletics. Ford won eight straight ball games with his baffling pitches, and his name was mentioned in the same breath as Cy Young and the other great hurlers of the era. He finished the season with a 26–6 record and a sparkling ERA of 1.65. The next season he won 22 and lost 11.

He might have gone on to compile Hall of Fame statistics, but a sore arm troubled him over the next few seasons and he lost more games than he won.

At that point his secret was out. A teammate caught him scuffing the ball one day, and when the teammate was traded to Cleveland, he told a pitcher on the Cleveland staff how Ford's scuffing of the ball was the secret to his success. The Cleveland pitcher, an eight-game winner during the previous season, began throwing scuffed baseballs and his record shot to 23–10.

By then all of the clubs had heard of Ford's use of emery cloth, and batters around the league howled in anger as more and more hurlers, assisted by the emery patches, caused them to flail their bats in frustration. League president Ban Johnson stepped in and banned the pitch. Umpires were ordered to scrutinize the balls for cut marks and scuffed surfaces. With the emery pitch outlawed the furor subsided. But even today, more than 80 years later, wily pitchers still find ways to doctor baseballs.

Russell Ford, the first man to do it, would be proud of them.

Curveball Candy Cummings

IN BASEBALL'S EARLY DAYS many games turned into slugfests, and 60, 70, even 80 runs in a game was a common occurrence. But the invention of the curveball soon made run scoring a batter's dilemma.

A pitcher named William "Candy" Cummings (1848–1924) is acknowledged as being the inventor of the curveball. People came from miles around to see Candy throw his curves for the old Brooklyn Stars. Most of them went away shaking their heads in disbelief, for pitching curves was contrary to nature, they said. Others, university professors and scientists among them, simply scoffed and said pitching curves was impossible. It was nothing more than an optical illusion.

Finally in 1877 in Cincinnati a test was made under scientific conditions. Three posts were set up in a line. Will White, a curveball pitcher, stood at the end of the line. Onlookers were amazed when White threw a ball that passed the middle post on the right side and curved around the final post on the left side. The doubting Thomases retired in confusion. They had seen it, but they still didn't believe it. Over half a century later *Life* conducted more scientific tests involving high-speed cameras to prove that curveballs could be thrown.

"Personally I'm not certain whether a ball curves or not," Eddie Sawyer, a former manager of the Phillies, once said. "But I am certain there is a pitch in baseball much different from the fastball that separates the men from the boys. If this pitch doesn't curve, it would be well to notify a lot of baseball players who were forced to quit the game they loved because of this pitch, and may be reached these days at numerous gas stations, river docks, and mental institutions."

Stolen Base King No Match for the Flint Flash

ON MAY 1, 1991, the Oakland Athletics' Rickey Henderson made a headfirst dive into third base and created baseball history with career steal 939 — a major league record. The former mark was held by Lou Brock, who witnessed Henderson's record theft and walked out onto the field to congratulate him.

"Rickey, you might be the greatest competitor that ever ran the bases," Brock said. "You are a legend in your time."

Henderson was saluted with a five-minute ovation after his historic steal in the fourth inning against the Yankees. He rose from the dust at third, yanked up the base as a souvenir, held it above his head, and pumped his fist in the air.

Modesty deserted him when he was asked to address the 36,000 fans in the Oakland Coliseum. "Lou Brock was a great base stealer, but today I'm the greatest of all time," he boasted. Later, when the A's presented him with a Porsche in recognition of his feat, he was reported to have said, "I'd rather have a Mercedes."

In Phoenix, Arizona, a former professional ball

player named Sophie Kurys scoffed at Henderson's record. Kurys, known as the Flint Flash when she played in the All-American Girls Professional League from 1943 to 1952, stole a whopping 1,114 bases.

And don't tell Kurys, now in her late sixties, that her record doesn't count because she played in a women's league. "We were a major league," she says, "and we played just as hard as the men. And because we played in skirts, I got plenty of strawberries from sliding into bases. Wouldn't you know a man designed our uniforms. A lot he knew."

Kurys's top salary was $375 per week, but she earned a $1,000 bonus in 1946 when she hit .286, stole 201 bases in 203 attempts, and was named player of the year. She set her base-stealing record in 113-game seasons, compared with the 162-game seasons played by today's major leaguers.

McCormick Loses Same No-hitter Twice

IMAGINE HOW MIKE MCCORMICK feels about his journey into and out of the record book. He has done it a few times. One dates back to a 1959 game in Philadelphia in which the San Francisco Giant southpaw was sailing through five innings of no-hit ball against the Phillies. His teammates had staked him to a 3–0 lead.

In the bottom of the sixth, however, Richie Ashburn, the Phillies' superb outfielder, singled. Having lost his no-hit bid, the 20-year-old McCormick proceeded to walk the bases loaded. Rain descended on old Connie Mack Stadium at this point, and eventually the game was called with the score and all records reverting to the last complete inning at the end of the fifth. At that point, however, McCormick still had his no-hitter. The game was thus ruled as completed, and in keeping with the practice of the day McCormick got his no-hitter back.

The no-hitter remained intact for over 30 years until a major league rules committee decided that all such shortened no-hitters would no longer be officially recognized. So the unfortunate McCormick lost his no-hitter for the second time.

McCormick wasn't the only Giant hurler to lose a no-hitter in this manner. In September of the same season Sam Jones spun a seven-inning no-hitter against the Cardinals, but the game was stopped by tornado-type winds in the eighth.

McCormick's and Jones's fates however are nothing in comparison to that of the hurler who tossed 1959's most famous no-hitter. Pittsburgh's Harvey Haddix dazzled the baseball world by not only pitching a no-hitter but a perfect game for 12 innings. No batters reached base until the 13th inning when both the no-hitter and perfect game were broken up and the Pirates lost 1–0.

Harvey Haddix's day in the sun was memorialized as a 12-inning gem until the rules committee blanked it from the perfect game and no-hitter record book.

Baseball by the Numbers

IN 1888 THE CINCINNATI REDS were asked to wear numbers on the sleeves of their uniforms as an experiment. But the players complained vehemently, claiming the numbers detracted from their identity as humans and athletes. So the numbers disappeared. In 1916 the Cleveland Indians stitched numbers on their uniforms, and in 1924 the St. Louis Cardinals followed suit. But the fans complained that the numerals made the players look like convicts. Once again the numerals vanished.

Resistance to a numbering system by players and fans meant that ball players went unnumbered until 1929 when the New York Yankees adopted the practice. The Yankees had the numbers coincide with their batting order. Thus, Earle Combs was handed 1, Mark Koenig 2, Babe Ruth 3, Lou Gehrig 4, and Bob Meusel 5.

Ruth quickly made his number 3 so renowned that many latter-day fans swear he was wearing it the day he hit his 60th home run. But he wasn't. His record blast came on September 30, 1927, two years before he wore any number at all.

The last team to hold out against numbering its players was Connie Mack's floundering Philadelphia Athletics. The 1930s were almost at an end before Mack caved in. Some say his players resisted numbering because of their pathetic play. Numberless jerseys provided anonymity.

Some ball players request certain numbers for specific reasons. You can guess what number Bill Voiselle, a pitcher for the Giants and the Braves in the 1940s, requested after he listed his home town as Ninety-six, South Carolina. Others wear their birth dates on their backs. When catcher Carlton Fisk was traded from the Red Sox to the White Sox, he thought it represented a change in his career, so he turned his number around, from 27 to 72.

Prior to the 1983 season pitcher Frank LaCorte

decided to get rid of his number 31. "It reminded me of a three-and-one count," he said. So he burned his uniform and settled for number 27. Later he had a change of heart, reclaimed number 31, promptly developed calcium deposits, and was out for a year. And there have been at least three ball players who wore 00 — Bobby Bonds, Paul Dade, and Otto Velez.

The oddest number, or noninteger, ever given a ball player was ⅛. It covered the back of three-foot, seven-inch Eddie Gaedel, the famous midget who went up to bat for Bill Veeck's St. Louis Browns on August 19, 1951.

Baseball's First Slider

WHILE SKIMMING THROUGH the library microfilm of the 1907 baseball season, I came across a statement from an old-time fan who had witnessed games 40 years earlier. Who, he was asked, was the first ball player to slide into a base, thus avoiding a rival infielder's tag?

"Fellow named Tim Murnane is often given credit as the originator of the slide," the old-timer stated, "but it ain't so. The first slider was Tim Studley, a

Tim Studley was baseball's first slider. He would slide 15 or 20 feet into a base on his stomach.
(Virginia State Library)

100

player with the Washington Nationals who introduced the strategy in the season of 1867.

"Studley tried it in a game that season between the Nationals and the Eurekas of New York. I was there when the stunt was pulled and the crowd roared with glee. Some of them thought Studley had slipped while racing to the base, and by sheer accident beat out the throw, but when Studley later repeated the feat, the daring base runner was loudly cheered for 'his bravery.'

"Nick Young, the former president of the Washington club, informed me recently that there was no doubt Studley was the pioneer of the slide. He was the first to slide 15 to 20 feet on his stomach to a base, claiming that it was going against the grain to slide in feet first. In those days the catchers did not throw low to the base, and Studley had no trouble in sliding into the base safely almost every time he tried it."

Short Porches

NOTHING IS MORE APPETIZING to a hitter than a short distance to an outfield fence. The Boston Red Sox have broken the hearts of their left-handed pitchers for years because of the nearness of the Green Monster in left field. Meanwhile their batting lineup has often sagged under the predominance of power-hitting right-handers who went into prolonged slumps away from the friendly confines of Fenway.

The Monster's intimidating presence, however, can't compare with the thrill a batter must have felt stepping up to the plate in Lake Front Park in Chicago in the last century. Home of Chicago's National League team in 1884, the park was a long ball hitter's paradise, measuring a scant 180 feet from home plate to the left-field foul pole, 196 to right, and 300 feet to center.

The park's Little League dimensions revolutionized the sport for that one season. Until then a home run was a rarity because most parks were like open fields. But that year four Chicago players hit over 20 homers, including Ed Williamson (27), Fred Pfeffer (25), Abner Dalrymple (22), and Cap Anson (21). Put in perspective, the rest of the league's players managed only 323 homers.

Batters didn't see such friendly dimensions again until the Dodgers moved west in 1958. With their new park in Chavez Ravine still to be built, they were forced to play in the Los Angeles Coliseum. Pitcher Sandy Koufax once described the Coliseum as looking like "the Grand Canyon with seats."

Although it seated 100,000, the stadium, built for the 1932 Olympics, was uncomfortably aligned to hold a baseball field. Accordingly the left-field fence was only 250 feet away from home plate. Wally Moon, an opposite-field hitter, mastered the art of poking innocent fly balls over the inviting target, hitting 19 in 1959. Right-handed pull hitters, by contrast, tended to swing from the heels and were easier targets for a pitcher with a good change-up.

Shortstop Pee Wee Reese claimed the Dodgers could sit out their left fielder and rely more on him. "Hell, I'll just backpedal a little farther than usual," he said, "just drift back until I feel the wall." For a few years this gifted survivor of the old Brooklyn Dodgers from the early 1950s was known to his teammates as "the drifter."

Putting More Color into the Game

WHY NOT ORANGE BASEBALLS? That was the question rebellious owner Charlie Finley asked his lodge brothers in the 1970s. Charlie had consulted with engineers who convinced him that orange balls could be followed in flight easier than the standard white ones. And he was probably right. But his fellow owners, already miffed at Charlie for draping his Athletics in gaudy green-and-yellow uniforms, voted him down. No orange baseballs, they said.

Charlie probably didn't know his idea had been tried before. Orange balls arrived in the big leagues in 1939, the same year as the first televised game. Both innovations were introduced at Ebbets Field in Brooklyn.

A year earlier orange baseballs had been used in games in the Western International League, with the fans and most players endorsing the idea. Oh, there were isolated cases of players complaining that they lost the flight of the ball because of its color, but they might have been looking for excuses for dropping it or not being able to hit it. When one batter was hit and injured by an orange ball, he beefed so loudly that sensitive league officials hastily brought back the white ones.

In the Brooklyn experiment a year later there

were no complaints about the visibility factor. However, players did mention a noticeable difference between handling orange balls and white ones. They said the colored balls had "a different feel." The manufacturers of the colored balls admitted the dye used to color the balls wasn't ideal, that it could rub off on palms that perspired, and that colored balls probably did have a different feel than white ones.

That was enough to cancel further use of orange balls. And reason enough, decades later, to reject Finley's proposal to reintroduce them to major league baseball.

Anson Refused to Strike Out

ADRIAN "CAP" ANSON MAY HAVE BEEN the smartest hitter of all time. Certainly he holds one record that nobody is likely to eclipse or even approach.

At the peak of his career in 1878 Anson, also known as Pop, struck out a couple of times during a spring training game. His Chicago White Stocking teammates kidded Pop because he seldom fanned. "Listen," he said, somewhat annoyed, "I was just horsing around out there today. I could have whacked the ball if I'd wanted to."

"Sure, Pop, sure," they jeered.

"Okay, wise guys. Here's what I'm gonna do," Anson roared. "I'll bet you $500 that I can play the regular season without striking out once."

The bet was accepted, and Anson played 102 consecutive games without striking out once. In the

103rd game he was whiffed on a questionable called third strike, one that everybody but the umpire thought was out of the strike zone. Even the rival pitcher shook his head in disbelief when the call went his way.

Anson didn't strike out again for the balance of the season. It was a near-perfect performance, so impressive that his teammates let him off the hook for the $500. Not surprisingly, the astute Anson amassed 3,041 career hits and ended his playing days with a .333 lifetime batting average.

Two-sport Hero Is Tossed Before He Plays

PLAYING ONE MAJOR LEAGUE SPORT well is difficult; playing two or more is almost impossible, and we marvel at the skill of those who attempt it. For some two-sport athletes, like Bo Jackson, the physical stress proves to be their undoing. Not so as yet for others, like "Prime Time" Deion Sanders, who shuttles back and forth between Atlanta's pro teams in baseball and football.

Ernie Nevers, the "one-man gang" for Stanford, played many seasons for the Duluth Eskimos and Chicago Cards of the National Football League beginning in 1926. He also played baseball with the St. Louis Cardinals as a pitcher from 1926 to 1928, and basketball with the Chicago Bruins of the American Basketball League at about the same time.

In Canada between the wars Lionel "Big Train" Conacher played professional lacrosse, starred in the Canadian Football League, and was a popular member of the New York Americans hockey club in the NHL. He also played minor league ball in Toronto, wrestled, boxed, and quite simply was one of the most amazing sports phenomena of his time. The most successful crossovers have been between basketball and baseball. Practitioners include Gene Conley, Dave DeBusschere, Del Rice, Lou Boudreau, and the late Chuck Connors. The latter once claimed he realized every kid's dream in the fifties, not only as a professional two-sport athlete but later as star of the television series *The Rifleman.* And before Dave Winfield turned pro he was drafted by three professional sports — football, basketball and, of course, baseball.

Missing from the above list is the great Boston Celtics star Bill Sharman. Called up by the Brooklyn Dodgers in late September 1951 after hitting .286 at Forth Worth, Sharman was on the bench as the frazzled Dodgers saw their once imposing lead over the New York Giants wither away. Playing in Boston on September 27, the Dodgers erupted when a Braves runner was called safe at the plate with what turned out to be the winning run. Plate umpire Frank Dascoli tossed out catcher Roy Campanella and coach Cookie Lavagetto, but the turmoil continued.

Finally Dascoli cleared the Dodgers' dugout and among those taking an early shower was Sharman. He never did make it into a major league game, and he is quite possibly the only player tossed from a game who never played in one.

Most Valuable Baseball Card

HALL OF FAMER HONUS WAGNER, the bow-legged shortstop of the Pittsburgh Pirates from 1900 to 1917, is perhaps more famous for trying to stop production of a baseball card than for a lifetime batting average of .329. Only a handful of his 1910 Sweet Caporal cigarette baseball cards were printed before he successfully stopped the print run. Those few cards are now legendary in the collecting world and have gained in value every year.

In 1989 Leland's Auction House sold a Honus Wagner card described as in "very good" condition for $115,000. Sotheby's topped that in 1991 by auctioning a mint Wagner card for a record $451,000. The winning bidders were Bruce McNall, owner of the Los Angeles Kings, and hockey star Wayne Gretzky.

Almost as highly sought is Mickey Mantle's 1952 Topps card. Topps put out 407 cards that year, but of the four series issued, the last one, which included Mantle's card, received limited distribution. The card wasn't even Mantle's first, that one having appeared before in the Bowman set. Today its value surpasses $25,000.

Another rare and valuable card is a 1916 Zeenut Series release of Jimmy Claxton of the Pacific Coast League's Oakland Oaks. Of mixed Irish, English, black, French, and Indian blood, the Canadian-born Claxton was fortunate even to have been playing in the league. In that era players with even a trace of black heritage were unofficially barred from any level of organized baseball and would remain so until Jackie Robinson broke the color barrier with the minor league Montreal Royals in 1946.

Claxton spent most of his career with a number of Negro league teams but signed on with Oakland after he presented them with an affidavit stating that he was a native American from a reserve in North Dakota. The Canadian southpaw pitched only one week in Oakland, but it happened to be during the time that a photographer was taking pictures for the 1916 set of Zeenut cards. The cards were released that year by the San Francisco-based candy company with Claxton's card among them. Only a few cards remain, and estimates place their value at over $1,000 each.

Zeenut cards were issued between 1911 and 1939, making them the longest-running continuous series of baseball cards until Topps and their famous Mickey Mantle card came along in the fifties.

Red Sox Flop as Trailblazers

THE BROOKLYN DODGERS ARE CREDITED with breaking baseball's color line. They signed Jackie Robinson for their Montreal farm team in October 1945, and the following year Robinson promptly stole 40 bases and won the International League batting championship with a .349 average.

Then, in 1947, he made history in Brooklyn when he became the first black major leaguer. It was the start of a sensational career that saw him win the National League batting title with a .342 average in

The Boston Red Sox gave Jackie Robinson a tryout even though they had no intention of signing a black player. (National Baseball Library)

1949 and eventually become the first black elected to the Hall of Fame.

What isn't known about the color line in baseball is that the Boston Red Sox might easily have become trailblazers, but they missed the opportunity. Two years before Robinson made his debut in a Dodger uniform, the Red Sox invited three blacks to their tryout camp. They were Marvin Williams, Sam Jethroe, and the multi-talented Jackie Robinson.

The tryout was a sham. The three blacks were there only because of a Sunday baseball bill before the state legislature. An important politician said he'd support Sunday baseball but only if the Sox would give tryouts to black ball players.

The Red Sox made the promise and gave the tryouts, but they had no intention of signing the players. Of the three black players they shunted aside, only Williams failed to make the majors. In time Jethroe became a respectable big leaguer and

Robinson became the most famous black player of the postwar generation, but with a more progressive organization.

Wildest Pitch on Record Made by a Canadian

ON THE AFTERNOON OF AUGUST 1, 1948, while pitching against Detroit, Canada's Phil Marchildon, a star with the Philadelphia Athletics, made history by uncorking what is conceded to be the wildest pitch ever seen in the major leagues.

Phil later admitted he was having control problems that day. He did indeed. In one inning he walked the first two batters, plunked the third in the ribs with a fastball, and walked the fourth man. Then, with a Detroit infielder at bat, Marchildon got the sign for another high, hard one. He took dead aim on the catcher's big mitt, wound up, and fired.

At that very moment, over in the grandstand, halfway between third base and the plate and about ten rows back, a gentleman named Samuel Wexler from Toledo, Ohio, happened to drop his scorecard. As Wexler bent down to retrieve it, Marchildon's pitch caught him squarely on top of the head, resulting in a huge welt and a period of dizziness.

Despite the pain, once he realized what had happened, Wexler managed to howl some menacing words and wave a clenched fist at the astonished pitcher. However, he was soon consoled by a spectator in the next seat who pointed out that it was, after all, quite an honor to be on the receiving end of what was undoubtedly the wildest pitch in baseball history.

Diamond Nicknames

BALL PLAYERS HAVE GREAT NICKNAMES, don't they? When I was young, I was intrigued with players with names like Vinegar Bend Mizell, Pee Wee Reese, Puddin' Head Jones, and Blue Moon Odum. And there were others known simply as "Babe," "Satchel," "Moose," or "Casey." Today, if a player doesn't have a suitable nickname by the time he reaches the majors, sports announcer Chris Berman is apt to find one for him.

Berman has singled out the following for his personal christening. Catcher Tony "Jala" Pena, shortstop "Fettuccine" Alfredo Griffin, left fielder George "Taco" Bell, third baseman "Hound Dog" Presley, first baseman Eddie "Eat, Drink, and Be" Murray, and pitchers Bert "Be Home" Blyleven and Kevin "Totally" Gross.

Two of Berman's favorite managers were Jim "Bela" Fregosi and Cookie "Days of Wine And" Rojas. Among his other all-time favorites are John

Reggie Jackson's World Series heroics earned him the nickname Mr. October. (National Baseball Library)

"Let It Be" Lowenstein, Von "Purple" Hayes, Wally "Absorbine" Joyner, José "Blame It On" Rijo, Harold "Growing" Baines, Walt "Three Blind" Weiss, Sammy "Say It Ain't" Sosa, and Chuck "New Kids On" Knoblauch.

When did Berman first begin Bermanizing major league stars? "It was in 1979," he recalls, "when I referred to Frank Tanana 'Daiquiri.' The name just slipped out, and they've been slipping out ever since."

The Youngest Player Ever

THE YOUNGEST PLAYER EVER to appear in a major league uniform in this century was 15-year-old Joe Nuxhall, star left-hander of the Hamilton, Ohio, high school team in 1944, the season he was spotted by a Cincinnati scout. During the war years, teams were desperate for players and age was no barrier to teenagers seeking big league positions.

On June 10, 1944, the Reds were being trounced by the Cardinals, and when the score reached 10–0, Reds manager Bill McKechnie told young Nuxhall to warm up. "It's time we got a look at your stuff against big leaguers," he said to the youngster.

Nuxhall went to the mound to pitch the ninth inning. He walked the first batter, then retired the next two Cardinals. McKechnie was just about to give the rookie the thumbs-up sign and a nod of approval when the kid started to come apart at the seams. He walked four more batters, allowed two singles, and was charged with a wild pitch. Before

McKechnie sent another relief pitcher into the game the score was 15–0.

Nuxhall's unique debut destroyed whatever confidence he might have had and he spent the next eight years in the minors. Finally, in 1952, he resurfaced with the Reds and quickly established himself as one of the most reliable southpaws in the National League. He played for 16 years and finished with a 135–117 mark.

The youngest pitcher to start a major league game in this century was Jim Derrington of the White Sox, a 16-year-old who hurled six innings against the Kansas City Athletics in a losing cause in 1956. In the game Derrington became the youngest player to hit safely in an American League game when he singled in two trips to the plate. Derrington pitched a few games for the White Sox the following season, then faded from the scene.

Let's Hear It for the Little Guys

IF THE AVERAGE NORTH AMERICAN MALE stands five feet, ten inches, baseball's little guys stopped sprouting well short of that standard. In some sports, like football and basketball, the peewee player doesn't have a chance. In baseball he can be a star.

So let's hear it for the players they call Mite, Flea, Shorty, and Topsy. Let's hear it for Kirby, as in Kirby Puckett who, at five-eight, often answers to Puck. During the 1991 season, Puck was awesome in leading the Minnesota Twins to a World Series victory.

In the past plenty of other little guys have emerged as World Series heroes. In 1947 an obscure Brooklyn Dodger outfielder, five-foot-six Al Gionfriddo, stole extra bases away from the Yanks' Joe DiMaggio with one of the greatest Series catches ever made. In 1951 it was another little Dodger, five-foot-eight Eddie Stanky, kicking the ball out of five-foot-six Phil Rizzuto's glove. In 1955 Sandy Amoros, five-seven, helped the Dodgers win with a Gionfriddo-like catch while the Yanks' Bobby Richardson, at five foot nine, was a one-man show in 1964.

Of the more than 1,000 players in the major leagues in 1992, 45 were under five-nine, enough to form a Small-Star Team, one that would acquit itself with distinction playing in any company. The title "shortest major league player in history" belongs to five-foot-one Pete "the Bug" Burg, who played a few games at second base for Boston in 1910. That is if you don't count Eddie Gaedel, the three-foot-seven midget owner Bill Veeck of the St. Louis Browns sent to the plate during a game in 1951. Compared to Gaedel, Burg was a towering figure.

Outfielder Albie Pearson, who played with Washington, Baltimore, and California from 1958 to 1966, was five foot five and may hold an unbeatable record — baseball's shortest rookie of the year. One manager, when he first glimpsed Pearson, asked, "What is this? Did Gaedel come back?"

Fred Patek, also listed at five-five, survived at shortstop for 14 major league seasons. After he retired, Patek confessed, "I lied about my height. I'm really only five-four."

Many little guys, like Puckett today, could hit the long ball. Hack Wilson, only five-six, belted 56 homers in 1930. Mel Ott, at five-nine, hit 511 in his career, and five-foot-seven Yogi Berra compiled 358.

Out of the thousands of players who have worn big league uniforms, only a handful have required a cut-down or batboy's version of the team uniform. Pete Burg, naturally, was one. Others requiring the skills of a tailor to alter pants and shirts were the 11 who played at five-three, the 23 at five-four, the 43 at five-five (including Hall of Famer Rabbit Maranville), and possibly the 154 who toiled at five-six.

Little guys who make it big, like Kirby Puckett, have sizable bank accounts. Three years ago the Twins, not noted for their largesse, signed Puck to a $3 million contract, making him, briefly, the highest-paid player in the game.

PART

5

DIAMOND DICTATORS

They Really Did Kill the Umpire

AN UMPIRE'S LIFE isn't an easy one. Players kick dirt on them, insult them, and say nasty things about their mothers. Furious fans spit on them, throw all kinds of objects at them, and physically assault them from time to time. It's a wonder, in big league baseball, when fans shriek, "Kill the Ump!" that some lamebrain hasn't done so.

Unfortunately in minor league ball at least two umpires have been killed in the line of duty. In 1899 Sam White, the plate umpire in a minor league game in Alabama, came under severe criticism from the crowd and the players on both teams. After White made a questionable call, one of the most vocal of the players rushed up to him, raised a big fist, and threatened to beat him up. White's reply was a punch to the player's mouth, sending him sprawling. When he got up, the player went berserk. He grabbed a bat and struck White viciously on the head, killing him on the spot.

A similar fate befell umpire Ora Jennings in a game played in 1901 in Indiana. An enraged player struck Jennings over the head with a bat, killing him instantly.

A Legend Looks Back

CONNIE MACK, WHO WAS KNOWN as baseball's Grand Old Man when he managed the Philadelphia Athletics many years ago, often reminisced about his playing days with the Washington club of the National League.

Mack's catching career began back in the 1880s, and he talked of an era when players caught the ball bare-handed and catchers stood well back of the plate and took the pitcher's delivery on the first bounce.

In Mack's day the pitcher stood a mere 45 feet away from home plate, 15 feet closer to the batter than in modern-day baseball. The hurler stood on a rubber block five and a half feet long and four feet wide. When he was ready to deliver the ball, he would turn his back to the plate, then swing into a hop, step, and jump and whip it toward the plate from below his hip, as in softball. But from 45 feet away it sailed in fast.

The rule then was seven balls and three strikes, except for 1887 when batters were allowed four strikes. Believe it or not, the batter was allowed to order the kind of pitch he wanted. If he was a high-ball hitter, he would tell the umpire that was what he wanted, and the pitcher would be instructed to throw them up around the shoulders.

Mack says all that changed in 1887 when pitchers were allowed to throw the ball any way and anywhere they liked. Batting averages plummeted when high-ball hitters (like Mack) found they couldn't hit balls thrown low and away in the strike zone.

An Astonishing Choice to Start a Series

WHEN MANAGER CONNIE MACK of the Philadelphia Athletics named Howard Ehmke as his starting pitcher in game one of the 1929 World Series against the Chicago Cubs, the world of baseball was stunned. Ehmke was the last pitcher anybody figured would be assigned to such a vital game. He was a 35-year-old has-been who had pitched just 54 innings. Mack had ignored him for days, a clear signal that his career with the A's was all but over, and when the A's took their final road trip through the West, the lanky right-hander was left behind, as unwanted as a bad cold.

Mack refused to divulge his reasons for starting Ehmke, but the story leaked out through Eddie Collins, his much-respected assistant general manager. Collins revealed that Mack had soured on Ehmke during the season after he took him out of a game with the Yankees. Ehmke had been responsible for most of the 13 runs the Yankees had scored, including a bases-loaded homer by Babe Ruth. When Mack pulled Ehmke from the game, he said, "Howard, that's the last game you'll pitch for me until you come and tell me you're ready to pitch. You weren't ready today and you should have told me so."

After the series with the Yanks, the A's traveled West for a few days and Mack left Ehmke behind. Collins and the rest of the A's figured poor Howard was all washed up. The A's went on to wrap up the American League pennant and prepared to meet the Chicago Cubs in the World Series. On the morning of the first game Mack called a meeting of his players. He went over a few matters and then dismissed them. All of the players filed out of the room except Ehmke. The pitcher said quietly, "Mr. Mack, you told me to let you know when I'm ready to pitch."

"That's right, Howard. I did say that."

"Well, sir, I want you to know I'm ready right now."

Mack smiled. "That's fine, Howard. Then you'll start today against the Cubs."

Collins almost swooned. He couldn't believe Mack had said what he had. But he knew his boss was renowned for knowing his players. If Mack believed Ehmke could battle the Cubs and win, chances were that he would.

How did Emhke fare in the game? His fastball wasn't overpowering, but using a baffling assortment of curves and change-ups, he turned in one of the finest pitching performances in World Series history. Not only did he win the game 3–1, he fanned 13 of the Cubs, establishing a Series record for strikeouts, one that lasted for 24 years until the St. Louis Cardinals' Bob Gibson fanned 17 Detroit Tigers in 1968.

The ninth inning was his most memorable. An error and two singles led to the Cubs' first run. There were runners on first and third with two out when pinch hitter Chick Tolson stepped in and worked the count to three and two. Ehmke took a deep breath and threw a fastball. Tolson launched a mighty swing — and missed. It was Ehmke's greatest moment in baseball, and his last.

Problems for an Umpire

BILLY CARPENTER WAS a turn-of-the-century umpire who wrote a newspaper account of his weekend's work after a pair of New York State League encounters in 1902.

"Please listen to the terrible tale I have to unfold," Carpenter wrote. "My troublesome affair dates back to a game between Syracuse and Albany. To be proper, the game was played at Rensselaer, New York, where all the home games of Albany were played. To get there it was necessary to take a little steamer across the river, and then the trolley for a short distance to the ball field.

"The score was tied 1–1 at the close of the 10th inning with both pitchers going superbly. The first Syracuse player to bat in the 11th received a base on balls. The pitcher protested vehemently and the fans roared in disapproval. I warned the pitcher that a continuation of his complaint would result in his ejection. He told me that I didn't have the nerve to put him out and that if I did he would have me mobbed. Since the base on balls had already got me in difficulty, I decided to accept the challenge. I accordingly notified Mr. Pitcher that he could hike to the clubhouse. It looked for a time as if I would have to forfeit the game and award Syracuse the win, but I finally got the contest started again.

"On the very next pitch the man on first started to steal. The Albany catcher threw badly to second and the runner continued to third. As he approached the bag, he decided he would try to score, so he rounded the base at full speed. The third sacker, seeing the runner in flight, gave him the hip as he went by and sent him sprawling in the dust.

"I was watching the play closely, and when the runner got up, I motioned him to come home because of the interference. In the meantime the center fielder had recovered the ball and made a beautiful throw to the plate. The catcher was waiting for the runner with the ball in his hand and touched him out. Or so the crowd thought. There was a wild scene when it became evident that I had allowed the run to score because the third baseman had flattened the poor fellow. The crowd became even wilder when the tally I allowed proved to be the game-winning run.

"With much difficulty I made my way to the dressing room where I found the president of the Albany club, the manager, and several other people awaiting my arrival. They all started at once to tell me what a crook I was. I tried to keep up my end of the conversation, but seeing I was hopelessly outclassed, I retreated.

"At the time it was customary in the New York State League for the umpires to be paid daily by the home team. Needless to say, I didn't get any salary that afternoon.

"After changing my clothes, I started off for the little steamer and noticed a huge crowd blocking the gangplank. They dared me to try to step aboard. A kindly chap with a rowboat offered to take me across the river. I accepted the invitation, but some of the crowd following me closely got wise. Just as I was about to step into the boat, I received a shove that sent me into the water up to my neck. I grabbed the side of the boat and managed to pull myself into it. As we started to pull away, we were given a shower of mud and stones.

"That evening the president of the Albany club sent a messenger over with my day's pay. It was seven dollars — all of it in pennies. The messenger also told me that I had better not show up the following day. Despite this warning, I arrived on the scene to work the game, but I was refused admittance to the park. The manager of the visiting team (Ilion had replaced Syracuse) heard about this, took my side, and refused to let his team take the field. Only then was I allowed to enter and take up my position behind the plate.

"The game moved along without any trouble, and Albany won an easy victory. That evening I was lauded by all in attendance simply for showing up, after the way I had been treated 24 hours earlier, and I was told that I was a real umpire. After that Albany was always an easy city for me to work in. But only because I showed them I wouldn't be intimidated by the roughneck actions of the fans there."

Finley Fuels Free Agency Fight

CHARLIE FINLEY'S TENURE AS OAKLAND A'S owner was marked by the introduction of orange baseballs, softball-type uniforms, and a mule as a mascot. During his flamboyant reign, the team won three consecutive World Series (1972–74), but his real legacy will probably be a cantankerous style of ownership that helped pave the way for free agency and the high salaries he despised.

In the 1973 World Series, when two errors by Oakland's Mike Andrews allowed the Mets to beat the A's 10–7 and square their series at a game apiece, Finley immediately placed infielder Andrews on the injury reserve list. Future Hall of Famer Rollie Fingers was furious. "We want him [Andrews] back. He's a great guy to be around, the kind of guy who'd help you out in a jam," the save artist complained.

In 1973 baseball's reserve clause, which bound a player to a team for life, was still in force, and owners could do pretty much what they pleased. But this time Finley went too far and Commissioner

Bowie Kuhn, at the urging of Marvin Miller, executive director of the Players' Association, stepped in and refused Finley's request to sit out Andrews. Finley's revenge was to indicate that even if Andrews returned to uniform, he wouldn't play in the remaining games.

Episodes such as this strengthened the players' resolve to seek some form of free agency. The first crack in the owners' armor occurred a year later when a judge ruled that Finley had failed to live up to his contract with Jim "Catfish" Hunter. The 28-year-old right-handed ace of Oakland's staff became a free agent and sold his services to the New York Yankees.

By the time Finley cashed in his interest in the A's in the late 1970s, free agency had changed forever the character of baseball, not to mention the carefree days when owners like Finley ruled with the power of an omnipotent dictator.

Bobby Bragan Had Lots of Time for the Umpire

MILT DUNNELL, WRITING in the *Toronto Star,* tells of encountering Bobby Bragan in the press box at a Blue Jays game. Bragan, after seven decades in baseball as a player, coach, and manager, recently authored a book entitled *You Can't Hit the Ball with the Bat on Your Shoulder* and he was telling Dunnell a couple of stories he had forgotten to include.

Years ago, with Bragan managing, the Hollywood Stars were engaged in a torrid series with the San Francisco club. This was in the Pacific Coast

League. The clubs reached the 21st inning of a Saturday night game with no winner in sight. So both sides were ready to welcome the 12:55 Sunday curfew.

"In fact," Bragan recalled with a laugh, "the two pitchers — our guy Bob Hall and Two-gun Gettel of their team — were shakin' hands at home plate because everybody in the world knew what time it was."

Everybody except the umpire. He ruled that the game should continue. In the next inning Jim Marshall of the San Francisco club hit a three-run double. Game over.

The next night, with the same umpire calling balls and strikes, Bragan walked to the plate to give the umpire his starting lineup. For the occasion he wore wristwatches on both arms, wrist to elbow. And dangling from his neck was an old-time alarm clock. Then, without a word, Bragan turned over his card to the ump, who struggled hard to contain his laughter.

In another tale, despite his love and respect for Brooklyn Dodger immortal Branch Rickey, Bragan wasn't averse to annoying the old gentleman. When Bragan was managing a Dodger farm team at Forth Worth, he needed outfield help, but he couldn't get Rickey's attention. Rickey, whose frugality was less than a state secret, had even cracked down on the use of telegrams. Messages were to be sent by airmail. In emergencies a telegram might be permissable, but the words had to be kept to a minimum.

In one game Bragan had his pitcher batting sixth in the order, with all three outfielders batting behind him. He figured that would get the attention of head office. Fresco Thompson, Brooklyn's farm director, immediately sent Bragan a letter, telling him that if he intended to embarrass the Dodger organization, he had succeeded.

No outfielder arrived, but ten days later Bragan received a wire from Rickey: "Can you get by with present infield?"

Remembering the order about brevity, Bragan fired back a reply: "Yes."

At the time Rickey had 21 farm clubs and probably had forgotten the question he had asked Bragan. He sent another wire: "Yes what?"

This time Bragan blew the brevity rule. His return telegram read: "Yes, sir."

When Bragan tells you baseball was more fun in his era, you have to believe him.

Toronto Player Jailed for Kicking Ump

IT HAPPENED ON A HOT SUMMER day in 1907. Tim Flood, a player with the Toronto Maple Leaf baseball club of the International League, showed his displeasure over umpire John Conway's call in an unusual way. He ran at the arbiter and launched himself feet first into the man's chest. The astonished ump was knocked to the ground, gasping for breath, and took a few minutes to recover.

Meanwhile a police inspector ran onto the field and arrested Flood, charging him with assault. In court the following day Magistrate Dennison called the ball player before him.

"Mr. Flood, you are charged with committing an assault upon umpire John Conway in yesterday's ball game. Do you plead guilty or not guilty?"

"Guilty," the athlete replied.

Umpire Conway was then called to the box and asked to tell the court what had happened. "Oh, he jumped into me with his feet, Your Honor," Conway replied, reluctant to give evidence. "There were a couple of close decisions, and I guess maybe Flood was right to complain about them. The day was very hot and he was upset about being fined $50 and being thrown out of a game earlier this week."

The arresting officer was less sympathetic. He gave strong evidence against Flood. "The player ran at the umpire and jumped into his stomach with both feet," the officer said. "If Mr. Conway hadn't been wearing his chest protector, he would have been seriously injured. There has been too much of this rowdyism going on at the ballpark, Your Honor."

That was all the evidence that was needed. "You will go to jail for 15 days at hard labor," the magistrate ruled.

The harsh sentence drew a gasp from the spectators. President J. J. McCaffery and manager Joe Kelley of the ball club were speechless for a moment. As Flood was led away to the cells, his lawyer, J. Walter Curry, pleaded with the court. "Won't you make it a fine, Your Honor? This man is not a criminal."

"It was a criminal offense," the judge snapped. "There's been far too much of this violence in sport. We must put a stop to it. Next case."

Flood went below without a word. He was freed a week later and reported he had lost 10 pounds during his incarceration.

The Ump's New Shoes

OLD-TIME UMPIRE TIMOTHY HURST was a baseball legend. He never wore a mask or shin pads. Nor did he wear a chest protector. But he did sport a small cap on his noble head.

What's more, Timothy Hurst had no use for the spiked shoes worn by his brethren in blue. He preferred patent leather footwear, which he kept shined to perfection.

One day the distinguished arbiter appeared for a game in New York, wearing a new pair of patent leather shoes. He proudly took his position behind the catcher, knowing his shoes were the shiniest in the ballpark, if not in the entire city of New York.

A couple of innings went by, and suddenly Timothy Hurst made a call that sent New York Highlander manager Clark Griffith into a frenzy. Griffith ranted and raved and, in trying to kick dirt on Hurst, stepped all over his brand-new shoes. In due time play resumed, but not for long, because Hurst, while brushing off the plate, noticed that his new shoes were a shambles. Griffith's spikes had damaged them almost beyond repair.

"Time!" Hurst shouted, and the game was halted. Hurst left his post, walked straight into the Highlander dugout, took a cup, dipped it into the team water bucket, and began drinking. At the same time he turned toward Griffith, who stood, arms folded, a couple of feet away.

Suddenly, in mid-drink, Hurst's free hand flew out and his fist knocked Griffith backward over the bench. One onlooker described it as "a punch that would have made Dempsey proud."

"Well, back to work, boys," Hurst said, placing the cup back where he found it. Then he winked at the startled players and walked calmly back to home plate.

Perhaps only Hurst's temper was better known than his sartorial elegance. Once, after some spectators threw beer mugs at him, as they were wont to do, the angry umpire picked up one of the mugs and heaved it back into the stands, striking a fireman. Hurst was arrested, tried, and fined $20.

The Manager Was a Lady

THE 1992 COMEDY HIT *A League of Their Own,* which tells the story of the All-American Girls Baseball League, had no need to take liberty with the truth. Even the scene in which Geena Davis's baseball-playing character takes over the managing reins from her drunken field boss (played by Tom Hanks) has at least a partial connection to reality.

The women's league was started in 1943 by chewing gum magnate Phil Wrigley as a wartime diversion for fans disgruntled by the decline of major league baseball. It lasted until 1954. All of the league managers with one notable exception were men who had enjoyed successful major league careers.

Jimmy Foxx, one of the game's all-time great home run hitters. (National Baseball Library)

One of them, Bill Wambsganss, had made the only unassisted triple play in World Series history. And Jimmy Foxx, the model for Hanks's character, hit 534 career homers.

In 1950 there was an opening for a manager of the Kalamazoo Lassies franchise. "I had played most of my career with the South Bend Blue Sox as their catcher," Mary "Bonnie" Baker recalls, "but they sent me over to Kalamazoo in mid-season when their manager was fired. I finished the season as manager, and afterward they offered to extend my contract. But at a meeting in Chicago the league vetoed it. It seems they were concerned that it might embarrass the former big league stars if my team beat one of theirs."

Mary Baker appeared on the popular television show *What's My Line?* Not surprisingly, her unusual career path almost stumped the panel. Because she worked as a model in the off-season, she was the perfect league representative, being both skilled athletically and glamorous off the field, similar to the character played by Geena Davis in Penny Marshall's film.

"My husband was overseas," Baker recalled, "and it was a chance to make some money. During the war, my picture appeared in *Life* magazine. I got letters from servicemen all over the world. One fellow wrote to say that he had two daughters, and he hoped they grew up to look like me and do the things I'd done."

Following her unique career in baseball, Baker returned to her hometown of Regina, Saskatchewan, where she became Canada's first female radio sportscaster. Meanwhile baseball is still awaiting its second female manager.

PART

6

ASTOUNDING ANTICS

Brooklyn's Babe Greets
Two Teammates at Third

YOU COULD ALWAYS RAISE A SMILE in Brooklyn by telling a group of Dodger fans that their team had the bases loaded. "Which one?" they'd invariably ask.

In August 1926 in the first game of a double-header Brooklyn's Babe Herman batted with the bases full. He promptly hit the ball off the right-field wall, thus commencing one of baseball's most amazing occurrences.

It helps to know a little about the Babe. Born in Buffalo, New York, he got his start in organized baseball in Edmonton, Alberta, in 1921. Years later he fondly recalled that his teammates included the local hockey star Duke Keats, and a future major leaguer Heinie Manush, who hit a home run over the right-field fence on opening day. "They had movies of it and showed them that night at the theater," Babe later recalled.

There was always a theatrical, some would say slapstick, side to Herman's baseball career. A great hitter but woeful fielder, he was a man born too soon to benefit from the designated hitter rule. Once he carried a lit cigar in his pocket for an entire game. Another time a fly ball bounced off his head for a ground rule double.

Nothing, however, compared with that memorable game in 1926 against the Boston Braves. Following Herman's hit, Hank DeBerry scored from third, but pitcher Dazzy Vance on second tagged up, thinking the ball would be caught. By the time he rounded third, the ball was already on its way to the plate, so he retreated to the bag. There he was

137

Brooklyn's Ebbets Field, fabled home of the Dodgers before they moved west. On this diamond Babe Herman performed some of baseball's wildest antics.

(National Baseball Library)

greeted not only by Chick Fewster, who had advanced from first, but Herman himself, who knew the ball was a hit the moment it had left his bat.

For a brief, shocking moment there were three runners on third! As the lead runner, only Vance was entitled to remain. So Fewster and the Babe both headed back to second and were easily tagged out en route. After much head scratching, the official scorer's verdict was that Babe Herman had doubled into a double play.

A Memorable Ladies' Day

IN BASEBALL'S FORMATIVE YEARS the game was the dominion of men — and men only. Ladies were often restricted from attending games in which foul language and spitting were part of the action.

But in 1897 the owners of the Washington club decided to hold a Ladies' Day. Female fans were invited to watch the team perform, free of charge. The promotion was immensely successful as hundreds of women turned out. Most of them came to see the popular Washington pitcher, George Mercer, for he had the looks of a matinee idol.

Unfortunately Mercer also had a nasty temper, and when umpire William Carpenter made some calls that Mercer objected to, he berated the man. Mercer's many female fans supported him. Later, when Mercer put on a little show for the ladies by presenting the umpire with a pair of eyeglasses, they laughed and applauded. But Carpenter had had enough of Mercer and tossed him out of the game.

That triggered a wild reaction. The ladies were furious, and for the rest of the game they showered poor Carpenter with verbal abuse. When the game was over, they poured out of the stands and attacked the man, tearing his clothes and beating him with their parasols. Members of the grounds crew rescued him and dragged him into the Washington clubhouse where they bolted the doors against a barrage of debris.

Outside, the rampage continued as the women destroyed seats, broke windows, and kicked at the bases. Some of them stayed until dark, waiting for Carpenter to reappear. But the shaken arbiter was smuggled out a side door and ran for his life, thankful he hadn't been beaten to a pulp.

It was a long time before any of the other clubs resumed their special days for ladies.

Germany Schaefer Steals First Base

IF GERMANY SCHAEFER HADN'T BEEN a ball player, he would have made a great lawyer. He knew all the loopholes in the baseball rule book and used them to his advantage. He was often regarded as a bit of a clown, but there was always a method to his madness.

Joining the Detroit Tigers in 1905 (along with Ty Cobb), he pulled off one of the great, and at that time legal, stunts in baseball history. His team was tied with Cleveland after nine innings when Schaefer reached first. The speedy Davey Jones was perched on third. Germany signaled Jones for the double steal against sore-armed Cleveland catcher Nig Clarke. But Clarke refused to throw to second on the twin steal, and Schaefer took the base while Jones remained on third.

On the very next pitch Schaefer thrilled the fans and shocked Cleveland by racing back to first base. Having now "stolen" two bases and finding himself back where he began, Schaefer was prepared to try the original play again. This time a completely befuddled Clarke took the bait, and his errant toss to second allowed Jones to score the winning run while a laughing Schaefer slid in safely.

Aghast at such disrespect for the purity of baseball tradition, the stuffed shirts on the rules committee banned such behavior in future. The imaginative Schaefer, however, had other yarns to spin.

Later in his career he tried to convince umpire Silk O'Laughlin that a drizzle was cause for cancellation of a game in which the Tigers were hopelessly behind. He appeared at the plate with rubber boots, raincoat, and umbrella. "Show me in the rule book where it says I can't wear a raincoat and boots," he said to the protesting O'Laughlin. By the time he was ordered to doff his unusual gear, the rain had turned into a downpour, and to the relief of the Tigers the game was called.

Schaefer's gift for the comedic eventually led him onto the stage where he and Tiger shortstop Charley O'Leary were a popular vaudeville twosome for several winters. The MGM musical *Take Me Out to the Ball Game*, starring Gene Kelly and Frank Sinatra, was based on their hijinks.

Later, as a coach, he put his clowning into more serious perspective. "Comedy alone will not serve on the coaching lines," he said. "The real stuff must be worked in. Humorous coaching is valuable for two reasons — it keeps our fellows relaxed and it sometimes distracts the opposing players." Nig Clarke would have agreed with that assessment.

The Blue Jays' Spider-Man

SPIDER-MAN. IT WASN'T A NICKNAME he liked. In fact, he detested it because it reminded him of one of the most horrible nights of his life.

Outfielder Glenallen Hill was a member of the Toronto Blue Jays in 1990. He was asleep in his bed on the night of July 6 when he had a strange dream, which became a nightmare when spiders the size of dinosaurs began to attack him. Hill, who suffers from arachnophobia, a deep-rooted fear of spiders, leaped out of bed in panic. Only half awake and petrified, he crashed into the furniture in his apartment, breaking a large glass coffee table. Then, frantically, he crawled through the glass on his hands and knees, pursued by the poisonous spiders.

Finally Hill woke up. Trembling and perspiring, he breathed a sigh of relief. The ugly spiders were gone, and he realized he'd been having a dreadful nightmare. Then he felt the pain. His arms and feet were badly cut from the broken glass. His face was a mess and his head hurt. Doctors treated his injuries and ordered him to use crutches for a few days. The Blue Jays were forced to put him on the 15-day disabled list. And, although his teammates sympathized with him, they couldn't resist giving him a new nickname — Spider-Man.

The Doghouse Home Run

WE OFTEN HEAR ABOUT A BALL PLAYER being in his team's doghouse, but how often do we find a real doghouse playing a role in the outcome of a game?

Only in recent years have ballparks been equipped with fancy scoreboards. For the first half of this century most parks relied on a scoreboard keeper, an employee who fitted numbered cards into slots at the end of each inning to keep the spectators aware of the score.

In Philadelphia before the turn of the century a small structure resembling a doghouse was built at the base of the right-field wall and was used to store the number cards. In a game played in 1892 Philadelphia was leading Chicago 2–1 in the top of the eighth when Chicago's Cap Anson stepped up to the plate with two runners on base. He belted the first pitch into deep right field. The ball bounced off a flagpole, rolled along the grass, and disappeared into the doghouse.

Philadelphia outfielder Ed Delahanty raced after it and crawled halfway into the doghouse, only to get stuck in the opening. The fans, meanwhile, were on their feet as Anson and his teammates rounded the bases. Finally center fielder Sam Thompson, grasping Delahanty by the ankles, was able to free his teammate, but not before Anson had crossed the plate with a three-run inside-the-park home run.

Pitcher O'Toole Gets a Bad Licking

IN 1912 PITCHER MARTY O'TOOLE of the Pittsburgh Pirates was one of the top spitballers in the game. In those days the spitter was legal, and Marty had no reason to hide the fact that he was loading up for his next delivery. He would bring the ball to his face, work up some saliva, and lick the ball with his tongue.

It was a disgusting habit, and it took some chicanery by the Philadelphia Phillies to cure him of it. Phillie first baseman Fred Luderus took a small vial of liniment onto the field with him one day when O'Toole was pitching. When the ball was thrown his way, he made sure a dose of the liniment was spread over its surface. When the Pittsburgh side was retired, he'd place the liniment-covered ball next to the mound, ready for O'Toole's use in the next inning.

When O'Toole loaded up, his tongue came into contact with the liniment, and he began to sputter and spit. He choked and howled that his mouth was on fire. Finally, tears streaming from his eyes, he called for a relief pitcher and staggered off the mound.

Traded for a Canine

IN 1915 MORDECAI "THREE FINGER" BROWN, a former Chicago pitcher, took organized baseball to court, alleging that owners and managers were guilty of many wrongdoings against the players. Brown submitted affidavits containing evidence that at least two ball players had been traded for dogs. He swore that Joe Cantalone, manager of the Minneapolis club, at one time traded a professional ball player for a bulldog. He also told the judge that Roger Bresnahan, while managing the St. Louis club, traded a pitcher named Hopper to the Springfield, Illinois, team of the Three Eye League for a bird dog.

How does a manager explain to a player that he has been dealt for a dog? "Sure we got a mutt for you. It was all the other team would offer. But don't feel bad. It's a good mutt. Won 'best of breed' in the New York Dog Show. So, really, we traded you for a champion."

Stengel in a Hole

CASEY STENGEL, THE ECCENTRIC outfielder, doffed his baseball cap one day and a bird flew out. Everybody knows that story, and at least a dozen other Stengel anecdotes.

But there is one Stengel prank that isn't so famous. When he was a young center fielder toiling for the Giants, he was involved in an exhibition game one afternoon in some long-forgotten minor league ballpark. Few chances came his way, giving Stengel a chance to study his surroundings. Nearby he noticed a manhole, which seemed to be covering a deep hole in the field. Stengel guessed it was there to give the groundskeeper a way to check the drainage system.

When the crowd was distracted by a close play at first base, Stengel popped open the lid and jumped into the hole. Then, pulling the lid down behind him, he tilted it slightly so that he could keep an eye on what was happening on the diamond in front of him.

He was underground only a few minutes when an opposing player drilled a high drive to center. By then the fans were screaming that the Giants were missing a ninth player — their center fielder. Then, as if by magic, Stengel popped out of his hole and chased after the ball. He said he would have caught it, too, but by then the left fielder had raced into Stengel's territory and pulled it in.

These Ball Players Traded Wives

TWO DECADES HAVE PASSED and middle-aged baseball fans can still be found discussing the trade that topped all others — the deal between two major leaguers — Mike Kekich and Fritz Peterson — who traded wives. In the early 1970s, they were pitchers, and roommates, on the New York Yankees.

The story broke during training camp in 1973. Mike and Susan Kekich had become good friends with Fritz and Marilyn Peterson. The Kekich children got along well with the Peterson kids. But what started out as a warm friendship between two families quickly turned into something quite bizarre when the ball players found themselves strongly attracted to each other's wife.

Each wife felt a similar attraction for the other's husband, and before long the couples agreed to swap mates. Once the decision became public it created sensational headlines in all the newspapers. The two couples agreed that the children would switch households, as well. Even the family dogs were involved in the barter.

Susan Kekich quickly became Susan Peterson, but Marilyn Peterson, after showing early enthusiasm for the novel arrangement, backed off at the last minute and refused to become Mrs. Kekich.

In 1991 Marty York, a curious sportswriter with Toronto's *Globe and Mail*, decided to track down the former Yankees. York found Kekich living in New Mexico and Peterson in Illinois.

"My whole career went into a black hole after 1973," Kekich told York. "The four of us had agreed that if any one of us wasn't happy with the swap, we'd call it off. But when Marilyn and I chose to call it off, it was too late. The other couple had already gone off with each other."

Kekich was traded to Cleveland a few weeks into the 1973 season. He had a 2–5 record with a dismal 7.48 ERA when the Indians cut him. Shortly after Kekich was released the Indians traded for Peterson. He went on to play 11 big league seasons (he also played for the Texas Rangers) and finished with a 133–131 record.

"Fritz was never the same after the swap," former teammate Fred Beene told York. "He was hurt terribly by all the negative mail and calls he got. But he also became very, very happy with Susan."

Peterson, a 49-year-old realtor, had four children with Susan, and they were raised with the two girls he had with Marilyn. Kekich, after pursuing a medical career that floundered because his degree was obtained in Mexico, became an insurance examiner in New Mexico. Five years after the famous swap he remarried. Now 47 he and his wife have a six-year-old daughter, and he keeps in touch with the two daughters from his marriage to Susan. He has lost all track of Marilyn but has been led to believe she is alive and well.

Kekich had little more to say about the trade that rocked the sports world. "It happened a long time ago," he told York matter-of-factly. "A lot has happened to all of us since then. I don't think any of us wants to think much about it anymore."

Baseball Announcers Say the Darnedest Things

AS A BROADCASTER MYSELF, I have occasionally made unwitting, hilariously wrong comments into the microphone. Once, during a Toronto Maple Leaf hockey telecast, I referred to team captain Darryl Sittler as Darryl Hitler.

Another time, when I mentioned to Bill Hewitt, my partner in the booth, that Bobby Orr was a unanimous choice as a league All-Star, he replied, "That's right, Brian. Almost everyone voted for him."

Over the years baseball announcers Ralph Kiner and Gerry Coleman have won renown for their on-air errors. *Sports Illustrated* writer William Taffe compiled a list of a few of them, beginning with these Coleman gems:

- Padre reliever Rick Folkers is throwing up in the bullpen.
- Winfield goes back to the wall. He hits his head on the wall and it rolls off! It's rolling all the way back to second base.
- We're all sad to see Glenn Beckert leave. Before he goes, though, I hope he stops by so we can kiss him goodbye. He's that kind of guy.
- On that play we saw Graig Nettles leaping up to make one of those diving stops only he can make.
- Hi, folks, I'm Gerry Gross. No, I'm not. This is Gerry Coleman.
- If Rose's streak was still intact, with that single to left the fans would be throwing babies out of the upper deck.
- If Rose brings the Reds in, they ought to bronze him and put him in cement.

Kiner is famous for calling Darryl Strawberry Darryl Throneberry and Gary Carter Gary Cooper. Once he even called himself Ralph Korner. He renamed Mookie Wilson Hubie Brooks and Hubie Brooks Mookie Wilson. Another time he said, "Mel Ott is rounding third base," when in fact the runner was Milt May, whom Kiner confused with Ed Ott. Some of Kiner's other broadcast beauties include:

- Scott Sanderson was traded from Montreal on Pearl Harbor Day, June 7, 1983.

- Cesar Cedeno has pleaded innocent to charges of running into a car.
- Madigan hit a sinking liner to left, but it went right into the glove of Murphy in right.

Then there was this memorable exchange between Kiner and former catcher Tim McCarver, no slouch himself when it comes to on-air gaffes.

"Now I'll turn the microphone over to my good friend Tim MacArthur."

"Ralph, my name is Tim McCarver."

"What did I say?"

"You said MacArthur."

"Well, that was pretty close."

"Balk! Balk! Not Walk!"

WHEN BO JACKSON, the two-sport star, was a rookie with the Kansas City Royals in 1986, he faced 300-game winner Don Sutton. Jackson swung hard and missed on the first two pitches. Then he took a ball, and when Sutton failed to come to a complete stop before his next delivery, the umpire yelled, "Balk!"

Jackson dropped his bat and trotted down to first base. When the umpire waved him back and gave him a quizzical look, Bo said sheepishly, "Sorry, Ump. I thought you said, 'Walk,' so I did."

There was a more important communication breakdown that took place during a World Series game in 1933. The Washington Senators and the New York Giants were tied at one with Dave Harris of the Senators on second base. When a teammate singled sharply to center, Harris ran toward third.

The third-base coach waved him on, shouting, "Go! Go! Go!" But Harris slammed on the brakes and ran back to the bag, failing to score.

"I thought you were yelling, 'Whoa! Whoa! Whoa!'" he explained to the perplexed coach after the Senators lost by a 2–1 score.

How Evers and O'Day Fooled the Fans

JOHNNY EVERS, OF TINKER to Evers to Chance fame, was known as the Crab in his playing days because of his many conflicts with umpires, particularly Hank O'Day. When he retired from the game, Evers explained how he and O'Day often amused themselves, if not the fans, with a routine worthy of the best actors on Broadway.

Evers would go into the bag with a slide, knowing he was out by a country mile. Yet he would pop up like a bull terrier and stick his chin in Hank O'Day's face, apparently jawing about the injustice of it all. What he really was saying was, "Hank, you're dead right I was out. You're such a great umpire. That was a wonderful call."

Scowling at Evers, O'Day would turn his broad back on the great infielder and walk a few steps away with the player in pursuit. Then he would whirl, place his hands nearly together, and say, "John, that's how much he had you by."

Evers would stomp the ground, throw his cap down, and reply, "Oh, more than that, Hank. At least twice that much. I didn't have a chance."

By this time the crowd was in an uproar, some cheering and applauding, but most booing and hooting at Evers for his poor sportsmanship in crabbing over a decision that was so obviously fair.

Eventually Evers would dust himself off and start to move away. Then he would whirl around and walk back to O'Day. "By the way, Hank," he would say, "how's the folks? Everybody okay?"

"No complaints, Johnny. No complaints," the grim-faced official would reply.

Evers would move away again, spin once more, and fling a handful of dirt at the umpire's feet. "I'm mighty glad to hear it, Hank. Mighty glad. May they continue to enjoy good health. And the same to yourself."

On his way back to the bench he'd stop once or twice more to yell back to Hank little comments about the umpire's folks and the correctness of the decision just made. He said it was hilarious the way a crowd could be worked into a frenzy with such antics. The most difficult part of the performance was to get through it without bursting into laughter.

Strike by the Tigers

ON MAY 15, 1912, the Detroit Tigers were playing the New York Yankees at the Polo Grounds in New York. Detroit's Ty Cobb was being heckled incessantly by a fan in the grandstand and as the game wore on Cobb's patience wore exceedingly thin. He asked the New York manager to do something, since crowd control was the responsibility of the home team. But the Yankee manager just laughed at him, and the Cobb-baiting continued.

At last, after a white spectator called him a "half nigger," Cobb leaped into the stands, grabbed his tormentor by the throat, and began to punch, kick, and stomp the man. Ushers and police arrived and dragged Cobb away. The next day American League president Ban Johnson fined Cobb $100 and suspended him for 10 days. Although Cobb was one of the least-liked men in baseball — even most of his teammates detested him — the Tiger players rallied to his support. Either Cobb was allowed to play, they announced, or they wouldn't take the field.

Ban Johnson ignored this threat and forced a showdown. The Tigers were due to play the Athletics in Philadelphia on May 18. If Detroit couldn't field a team on that date, Johnson said, the club would be fined $5,000.

Detroit manager Hughie Jennings pleaded with his men, but they refused to play without Cobb. On the morning of the game with the A's Jennings signed up nine youths from Philadelphia's St. Joseph's College. The nine recruits were aided by two fortyish Tiger coaches who returned to active duty for the day.

Jennings didn't care if the newcomers had any talent. He was merely trying to avoid the fine by fielding a team. He and A's manager Connie Mack discussed the problem, and both agreed to cancel the game if the major leaguers walked out. But at the last minute, after looking over the motley collection in the visitor's dugout, Mack changed his mind and said, "Let's play ball."

One of the recruits was a 20-year-old junior at St. Joseph's College in Philadelphia, pitcher Al Travers. "I was studying for the priesthood, so I didn't have much time for baseball," Travers recalled. "And I wasn't much of a pitcher. The only pitch I knew how to throw was a slow curve, and I'd never completed a game in my life. The amazing thing was, I did all right against the A's until the fifth inning, trailing by only 6–2. Then the A's started bunting, and I knew nothing about fielding bunts. Neither did my third baseman, because he'd never played baseball before. Before the game was over I'd given up 25 hits and 24 runs — 14 of which were earned. We also made nine errors that afternoon."

The next day, at Cobb's urging, the Tiger regulars called off their strike and returned to the field. The nine instant major leaguers were paid off and released. Travers, the priest-to-be, was given $50, while his teammates received only $10 apiece. Only one of the college boys ever played in the majors again and that was only for a day. Strangely nothing was ever heard again of the catcher recruited for the bizarre game, college player Ed Irwin. He belted out two triples in three at-bats and ended his one-day big league career with a batting average of .667.

One Hell of a Homer

IT WAS THE FINAL DAY of the 1903 season and the Chicago White Sox were playing the Washington club. "In the ninth inning Chicago needed but a run to win," Washington outfielder Jack Hendricks recalled years later. "As for me, I was out in right field. Not far away from me, sitting back on a chair in the team clubhouse, was Jimmy Ryan, one of our star players, who was injured and unable to suit up. From time to time during the game old Jimmy would nod off, his chin dropping down on his chest.

"Suddenly a ball came flying right toward me, one of those low and tricky screamers that outfielders hate. This one took a downshoot as it approached me and bounced off my big toe. Holy Moses, did it hurt.

"It carried on, still at a mile-a-minute pace, and flew through the open clubhouse door. Jimmy Ryan was still sitting there, dreaming no doubt of base hits and stolen bases, or maybe even a cold beer, when that ball caromed off his head. He dropped like a sack of wheat as the ball rattled around in the clubhouse.

"By the time I limped over to track it down, Isbell, the batter, crossed home plate with the winning run. It was a hell of a way to hit a homer. He immediately spun around and, cackling with laughter, waved in my direction. I was hopping around on what felt like a broken toe, and Jimmy Ryan was crawling out of the clubhouse on all fours, asking if the train that had hit him was a freight or a passenger.

"Friends and teammates of mine said it was the funniest ending to a game they'd ever seen. In time even Jimmy Ryan and I were able to laugh about it."

The Surprise Potato Play

THE SUM OF ONE DOLLAR and a potato was the entrance fee to a Double A battle between the Williamsport Bills and the Reading Phillies on a June day in 1988. The game in Williamsport marked the retirement of sweater number 59, belonging to former Bills catcher Dave (Spud) Bresnahan. A capacity crowd of 3,500 turned out to see a reenactment of a play that made Bresnahan a baseball celebrity the previous season.

154

At the end of 1987 the Williamsport Bills were 27 games out of first place with two games left on the schedule. Bresnahan, behind the plate, was hitting a mere .148 and realized his career was almost at an end. But before he bowed out he wanted to give the Williamsport fans something to remember him for. So he purchased three big Idaho potatoes, cut the ends off, and carved them into spheres roughly the size of a baseball.

In a meaningless game with Reading a Phillie reached third base, and on an apparent pickoff play Bresnahan took the pitch and fired what appeared to be the baseball high over the third baseman's head and into left field. The runner trotted home, where Bresnahan, holding the baseball, tagged him out. What the runner had seen fly over his head at third was the potato.

Everyone was amused except the umpire, the Williamsport manager, and the opposing players. The umpire allowed the run to score, and manager Orlando Gomez yanked Bresnahan from the game, fined him $50, and released him two days later. In leaving, Bresnahan decided to pay off his fine in an unusual way. He dumped several bags of potatoes on manager Gomez's desk with a note that read, "Orlando, this spud's for you."

One year later, prior to a game with Reading, Williamsport general manager Rick Mundean added a postscript to the story. Bresnahan was called back for a reenactment of the incident, which had received international attention. Many of the original players were involved, including Reading player Rick Lundblade, the base runner who had been victimized by Bresnahan. Fans read tributes to the retired player, he was presented with the keys to the city, and his number 59 was retired, ultimately to be strung up on the outfield fence.

"Baseball purists say we shouldn't have given Dave such recognition because he made a travesty of the game," Mundean said. "But we think he did something that is the essence of baseball — he had fun with the game."

Bresnahan told reporters, "Yankee slugger Lou Gehrig talked about being the luckiest man on the face of the earth when he had his number retired. I feel even luckier because Gehrig had to hit .340 and play in more than 2,000 consecutive games to have his jersey honored. All I had to do was hit .150 and throw a potato over third base."

Bresnahan may not have known it, but he wasn't the originator of the peeled potato trick. Years earlier New York Ranger coach Roger Neilson, while managing an amateur ball team in Peterborough, Ontario, pulled a similar stunt with equal success.

Diamond Daffiness in Montreal

ON JUNE 6, 1978, the Montreal Expos and the San Diego Padres reached the bottom of the sixth inning with the Expos leading 2–0. Suddenly Olympic Stadium was plunged into darkness because of a power failure.

The players retreated to their dugouts, and within a few minutes some of the lights flickered back on, but only on one side of the field. More time elapsed and a few of the players, bored with the delay, decided to entertain the fans with some stunts, the zanier the better.

The Padres' Derrel Thomas started it off by trying to throw a baseball out of the stadium. When he failed in several attempts, he tried something easier, rolling balls down the third-base line from home plate to the bag. Then he chased after the balls and pretended he was an umpire who couldn't decide if the balls were fair or foul.

Teammate Ozzie Smith, famous for his acrobatic skills, ran from the dugout onto the field and performed a spectacular backward flip and a pair of cartwheels, earning a huge ovation from the more than 14,000 fans. When Warren Cromartie of the Expos tried to outperform Smith, he deliberately fell flat on his face, drawing an even bigger cheer.

More stunts followed, including a phantom infield drill performed by the Expos. The infielders, without a ball, fielded nonexistent grounders, made spectacular catches, and threw relays to teammates who leaped and sprawled while the fans cheered themselves hoarse.

When the cheering subsided, San Diego pitcher Gaylord Perry strolled to the mound carrying a big bucket of gunk, which he placed on the ground an arm's length away. One of the game umpires came out to frisk Perry, a signal to the crowd that the pitcher had a reputation for doctoring the ball. After a lengthy search, the umpire gave the innocent-looking hurler a nod of approval, patted him on the back, and turned away. Perry then reached into the bucket and pulled out a ball covered with gunk. He threw a dozen pitches to the plate, breaking off some of the most amazing curveballs ever seen and triggering another ovation from the fans.

By this time the delay was closing in on 70 minutes, electrical repairs were still unfinished, and the ball players had exhausted their repertoire of stunts and gags. There were few complaints when the game was finally suspended.